CONSULTANTS NEWS

Career Guide to the Top Consulting Firms

American Management Systems
Andersen Consulting
Aon Consulting
Arthur Andersen
Arthur D. Little
A.T. Kearney
Bain & Company
Booz-Allen & Hamilton
Boston Consulting Group
Cambridge Technology Partners
Computer Sciences Corporation
Deloitte Consulting
Diamond Technology Partners
Ernst & Young
Gemini Consulting
Hewitt
IBM Consulting Group
KPMG
McKinsey & Company
Mercer Management Consulting
Mitchell Madison Group
Monitor Company
PricewaterhouseCoopers
Towers Perrin
Watson Wyatt Worldwide

KENNEDY INFORMATION

© 2000 Kennedy Information LLC
Fitzwilliam, New Hampshire USA
Telephone: (800) 531-0007
Facsimile: (603) 585-6401

Published by Kennedy Information LLC
One Kennedy Way, Route 12 South
Fitzwilliam, New Hampshire 03447 USA

ISBN 1-885922-60-4

By: Michael Norris and Giles Goodhead

Edited by Marshall Cooper

Kennedy Information and its agents have used their best efforts in the collecting the information published in *The* Consultants News *Career Guide to Top Consulting Firms.* Kennedy Information does not assume, and hereby disclaims any liability for any loss or damage caused by errors or omissions *The* Consultants News *Career Guide to the Top Consulting Firms,* whether such errors or omissions result from negligence, accident or other causes.

About Kennedy Information

Kennedy Information is the leading source of intelligence on the consulting profession. The firm has tracked the industry for nearly 30 years through its flagship monthly briefing, *Consultants News*, as well as through *Global IT Consulting Report*, *Consulting* magazine, and *The Directory of Management Consultants* (an annual compendium of consulting firms in North America). The firm also maintains the industry super-site *www.ConsultingCentral.com*. Kennedy Information analysts and editors are regularly cited by the media, including *The Wall Street Journal*, *The New York Times*, *Business Week*, and *Forbes*. Kennedy Information is headquartered in Fitzwilliam, NH, and has offices in New York and Los Angeles.

Table of Contents

A Note About The Different Types of Management Consulting Services 1

Considering A Career in Consulting? 3
Understand How Firms Differ 3
Four Differences That Matter 3
Four Differences That Don't Really Matter 4
Wrap-Up 5
Matrix Time: Real Consulting Firms Compared 5
How to Ace a Consulting Firm Interview 7
Self-Test: Is Consulting For You? 10

Interpreting Each Consulting Firm Profile 15

Profiles of 25 Leading Consulting Firms 17
American Management Systems 19
Andersen Consulting 24
Aon Consulting 33
Arthur Andersen 37
Arthur D. Little 43
A.T. Kearney 48
Bain & Company 53
Booz-Allen & Hamilton 59
Boston Consulting Group 65
Cambridge Technology Partners 69
Computer Sciences Corporation 75
Deloitte Consulting 80
Diamond Technology Partners 86
Ernst & Young 91
Gemini Consulting 97
Hewitt 102
IBM Consulting Group 107
KPMG 110

McKinsey & Company 114
Mercer Management Consulting 119
Mitchell Madison Group (MMG) (A USWeb/CKS Company) 124
Monitor Company 129
PricewaterhouseCoopers 135
Towers Perrin 143
Watson Wyatt Worldwide 148

A Note About The Different Types of Management Consulting Services

The 25 firms profiled in this book are all management consulting firms, but the precise services they offer to clients vary considerably. As a starting point, it is useful to divide consulting services into four broad categories, or "buckets":

1. Strategy
2. Operations Management
3. Human Resources
4. Information Technology

Strategy consulting involves giving advice and counsel about corporate-level or business-unit strategies. What business should we be in? How do we compete? Should we diversify or focus on core activities? How do we fight (and win) against our competitors? Popularized by BCG and McKinsey in the 1960s, strategy consulting has for the last 20 years been seen as a kind of elite consulting, bought by top client managers for top dollar rates. The work can be rather conceptual and glamorous. Consulting teams are usually small. Individual consultants tend to be generalists, moving from industry to industry. Results are often hard to measure. In an increasingly technological world, the value of "pure" strategic advice is being reconsidered.

Operations Management consulting is the original form of consulting: figuring out how to improve the efficiency or productivity of how a business works. Fifty years ago, the craze was for time and motion studies. In the 1990s, the buzzword was reengineering. Whatever the name, there is always a need for practical, results-oriented, microeconomic consulting. Quite often, operations consultants are industry specialists, people who really know how to make a certain kind of company hum.

Human Resources consulting for many years focused on compensation and benefits advice. In recent years, as people have recognized the importance of attracting, motivating, and retaining high quality employees for a company, HR consulting has blossomed. It can overlap closely with operations work (e.g., getting an incentive compensation plan just right) or strategic consulting (e.g., competing based on superior customer service).

Information Technology consulting has been the engine of growth for the entire consulting industry in recent years, a trend that shows no sign of abating. IT consulting now accounts for one-half of consulting industry revenues. The industry's largest player, Andersen Consulting, has its roots in IT work. Today it is hard to think of a business problem whose solution does not involve technology or, more specifically, systems. A good part of systems consulting includes helping clients install or operate massive packaged software "solutions" such as SAP. Ten years ago, IT consulting was snubbed at by "pure" advisory consultants who called IT people "plumbers." Today, IT firms dominate the largest consulting firm lists, and quite a few IT consultants are multi-millionaires thanks to public stock offerings. Revenge of the nerds.

Some of the firms profiled in this book are easy to categorize as "pure plays." Boutiques like BCG, Bain, McKinsey and Monitor do just strategy work. The Big Five and Andersen Consulting get the majority of their revenues from IT assignments, but thanks to their sheer size, they run strategy groups that rival the boutiques in numbers. Then there are IT specialists like IBM Consulting Group and Cambridge Technology Partners. Firms like Hewitt and Aon concentrate on HR work.

But quite a few firms are true generalists. Booz-Allen and A.T. Kearney offer a variety of consulting services, including extensive operations and strategy work. Mercer is known for its large HR group as well as its strong strategy practice.

Since most of the firms profiled in this book are large, we recommend that you review each profile carefully to get a deeper sense of the full range of services the firm offers. Don't be too judgmental about the type of consulting you want to do. There's a great deal of overlap among consulting services these days.

Considering A Career in Consulting?

Understand How Firms Differ

This book is intended to assist students and professionals in making career choices by providing fact-based and honest profiles of 25 leading consulting firms. Our approach is to provide job seekers with the same facts and figures that Kennedy Information publishes for consulting firm partners, spiced up with lots of direct, no-holds-barred quotes from people who work in the firms themselves.

Consulting firms say, "people are what makes us unique." Who do they think they're kidding, when what actually confronts you across the silver tray of shrimp is a battalion of dark suits indistinguishable from yesterday's cocktail party hosts? Yes, it's hard to figure out the differences between major consulting firms. Most are highly successful, growing rapidly, boast impressive rosters of clients, and are staffed by ambitious and relatively young professionals. These days, every firm has a good story about "doing implementation" or about "blending strategies with systems." This is, after all, what the marketplace wants.

Differences do exist, even if they're hard to spot at first sight. The key realization is that some differences are much more important than others.

Four Differences That Matter

1. The most important thing is the gut feeling you will develop by spending time with each firm's consultants. Of course, the partners may be the most impressive, but since you'll be spending more time with the regular consultants, associates, and analysts, figure out if you'll get on well with the foot soldiers, not the generals. You'll start to discover which firms are "work hard and play hard," which are "work hard, then go home and play elsewhere," and which are "work super hard and love it." We're not aware of any successful consulting firms that don't have a "work hard" culture. If you don't enjoy complicated and demanding work, consulting is not for you.

2. Another significant difference is the mix of work at each firm between conceptual strategy creation (upstream) and more specific tasks for improving the efficiency of a client's operations (downstream). Neither end of the spectrum is intrinsically better than the other. Rather, it's a question of where you'll learn the most and where you'll fit in. Strategy consulting has long enjoyed a sense of glamour, but suffers sometimes from a lack of measurable impact. You could spend twelve months developing a corporate plan for a big phone company and then have your bold plans ignored.

3. Specialization is an important issue to consider. Some firms require you to pick an industry group or a functional area. Others allow you to pick only if you want to specialize. Still others prefer you to be a generalist. Being a generalist can be an excellent way to see a range of client situations, but sooner or later, most people tend to become expert in something. As a new recruit, you have to decide what path is best for you.
4. Consulting firms also differ in terms of the training they offer. As a general rule, the bigger firms offer the most formalized training programs. Smaller boutiques are more likely to assign you directly to projects. Almost everyone agrees, however, that consultants do most of their learning on the job, not in the lecture room.

Four Differences That Don't Really Matter
1. How fast can you get promoted, or make partner? Our company profiles provide typical career tracks, but bear in mind that consulting firms are highly meritocratic. This means that if you're smart and hard-working, you will jump ahead quickly at any firm. It would be misguided to choose one firm over another because the average time to partner was a year shorter.
2. We also recommend that students don't pay too much attention to starting compensation packages. Easier said than done, especially when that juicy signing bonus could wipe out your student loans. But you'll find that the differences between firms are typically slight. A two thousand dollar difference in your starting package becomes trivial over the course of your career. It's far more important to end up at a firm where you'll excel and be happy.
3. Some firms are growing more quickly than others. Over time, fast growth can mean greater opportunities for responsibility and advancement. Too fast growth, however, can mean excessive hours, thinly-staffed case teams, and overloaded internal support systems like mentoring and training. Take a long-term view on growth: A few percentage points in a given year between firms isn't meaningful to your career choice.
4. Lifestyle and travel are certainly important issues to consider. The trouble is, they're both hard to predict in consulting, and the differences tend to be from one project to another more than from company to company. At almost any major firm, you could end up commuting half-way across the country every week for six months until your friends no longer recognize you. As a rule of thumb, the more offices a firm has, the less long-distance travel should be required. Try asking firms what they view as normal or typical travel requirements. You can also look at the ratings each firm gets for "lifestyle" in the firm profiles. Bear in mind that these ratings are perceptions, not a measure of consultants' actual quality of life. As many of the quotes from consultants inter-

viewed for this book suggest, your lifestyle is something that you have to manage actively at any firm. That's the nature of being a consultant.

Wrap-Up

Focus on the kind of consulting work that you find interesting. Pay attention to what sort of role you can expect on a project team. Ask about training and specialization. Above all, try to get a feel for the culture: Would it be fun to work at this firm year after year?

Don't get obsessive about the short-term dollars, or the firm's standing in the *Consultants News* 50. Don't worry if your favorite firm is being sued by a client. (Almost every firm in this book has had legal squabbles with clients.) Don't be too impressed by brand names, although the best brand names are admired for good reasons. Don't pick the San Francisco office of a firm you dislike over an office elsewhere of a firm you love, unless it is imperative that you live in San Francisco (you'll probably be on a plane to somewhere else most Monday mornings anyway). Finally, do enjoy the shrimp cocktail and Chardonnay, but don't be taken in by fancy wining and dining. You'll tire of eating in restaurants soon enough.

Matrix Time: Real Consulting Firms Compared

The consulting profession is infamous for creating "two-by-two" matrices as a way of portraying a business issue. One of the most famous matrices was pioneered by The Boston Consulting Group (BCG) in the 1970s; the "Growth Share Matrix" was used by BCG (and then by everyone else) to profile the different business units in a large corporation (see Figure 1).

Figure 1

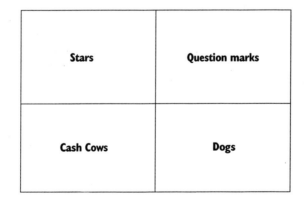

The market share of each business was measured along the horizontal (X) axis, while the growth rate of each business was measured along the vertical (Y) axis. For example, a business with a high market share and a high growth rate would appear in the upper left quadrant of this "two-by-two" matrix. Such a business was termed a "star." Low market share, slow growth businesses in the lower right quadrant were called "dogs." Consultants would usually recommend to their client that "the dogs be taken out back and shot." (Consultants love using animal and sporting metaphors in business.)

It's an interesting exercise to place consulting firms on their own two-by-two matrix. (Good practice for your interviews, too!) Figure 2 highlights some differences between firms along a couple of dimensions that are relevant to you.

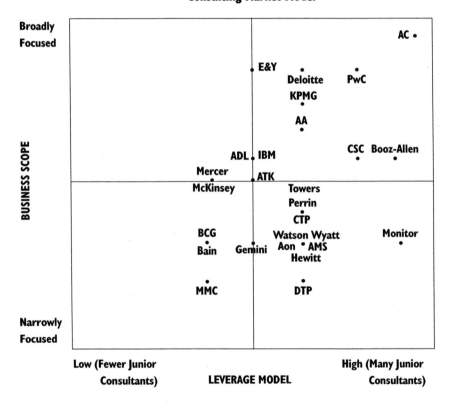

Figure 2

The horizontal (X) axis refers to each firm's "leverage model." Think of this as the shape of their employment pyramid. Some firms have high leverage: This means that they employ a large number of junior people for every partner. The implication for you as a new recruit is to expect large project teams with lots of entry-level consultants. The vertical (Y) axis refers to whether each firm is some kind of specialist or offers a "one-stop shop" of many consulting services. Compare Andersen Consulting (broad scope, does everything) and our two-by-two matrix popularizer BCG (narrow scope, focuses on corporate strategy consulting).

We've placed each firm profiled in this book on the matrix. The firms themselves may disagree with where they are placed. What's important is where *you* think they go and what kind of firm you feel will suit you best.

How to Ace a Consulting Firm Interview

The good news: Consulting firms are hiring by the thousands, desperate to add 250,000 warm bodies over the next three years to meet booming demand for their services. The bad news: Getting job offers from large, well-known firms is tough, even if you're highly qualified.

Consulting interviews are notorious. Nervous candidates can expect mathematical puzzles, complex case studies, and tests of teamwork to be flung at them in rapid succession. Why so brutal? Because McKinsey, Andersen Consulting, Mercer, and the rest are only as good as the people they recruit, and because a job as a consultant demands that you be intellectually rigorous and nimble, all while keeping your poise in front of clients paying six- or seven-figure sums for your wisdom. Here are four main types of interviews consultants use to test these skills, plus tips on handling each one.

1. *The classic case study*

"Let me tell you about a project I've been working on," says the dark-suited partner, smiling ominously. "Our client makes ring laser gyro-based inertial measurement units for fly-by-wire aircraft. It's been losing share recently and wants us to figure out why. What do you think?"

Of course, you haven't a clue. You don't even know what a ring laser gyro is. That's exactly the point here: You're not supposed to guess the right answer; you're supposed to ask the right questions. Don't worry about industry jargon. Start by asking questions like: "Who are the client's competitors and which ones are gaining market share from us?"; "Is the client losing share to all customers or just to some customers?"; and "Are the customers choosing other gyros because they're lower in cost or because they work better?"

The consultant is looking to see if you can think logically, absorb all the information he or she is throwing at you, and not get sidetracked or discouraged by blind alleys ("No, our client's gyros are just as good as everyone else's!"). Above all, stay calm.

Some people try to use clever consulting techniques (such as Five Forces, a framework for analyzing the profit potential of an industry, or the Four Ps, an analytical tool used in marketing) to help structure their approach to the case. These techniques work when they're relevant to the problem, but it's safer to use a common-sense method than to show off. It's also a good idea to jot down brief notes. All consultants worth their salt continuously take notes.

Interviewers want candidates who can think and perform complex analyses and be pleasant while doing it. Unfortunately, your interviewer may be a brilliant consultant, but there's no guarantee he'll be any good at conducting a case interview. Faced with a rambling consultant, try to get the discussion focused. Above all, don't get discouraged: Consultants love "tire biters."

2. *The fire-fight*

This is the interview where the consultant wants you to estimate the number of golf balls in America and then calculate 752 x 13 in your head. These questions are common in first interviews (sometimes referred to as "brain screens"), when consultants want to weed out candidates who aren't budding Mensa members. They're also used to test applicants whose degrees aren't in science, economics, or engineering.

Refuse to be flustered. Most problems are easier than they seem. To solve them, you must make assumptions and sensible guesses. In the prior golf-ball example, estimate what proportion of the U.S. population plays golf and how many balls average golfers have in their club bags. As with case studies, how you think is more important than producing right answers. (Nobody knows how many golf balls there are in America. In fact, probably nobody cares).

3. *We're so impressed*

A seemingly easy interview is often a deadly trap. Your interviewer immediately puts you at ease, telling you how impressive your reasoning skills were in the previous round. "Your resume is superb," he or she says. "So, what would you like to know about us?" Sounds like you've landed the job with twenty-five minutes left in the interview. Is it time to ask how soon you can expect to make partner?

No! It's another test. You have just been given control of a block of time. The interviewer wants to see how well you use it. This is equivalent to the moment in a meeting with clients when the consultant stands at the white board with a pen and two hours before lunch. What are you going to say? Boring questions about the consulting firm's history or ambitions will get you dinged.

It's far better to say something like this: "I'd like to spend about ten minutes each on three topics. First, your company's training programs—what are they, how seriously are they taken, and what skills they are designed to teach? Second, how do the day-to-day duties of an associate at your firm differ from those at competitors X and Y? Third, I'd be interested to hear how you came to choose this company, how your own career has evolved, and whether it's been what you expected. Shall we start with training first?" Done right, this sort of structured approach will get you a job offer every time.

4. Team games

You're in a room with three equally nervous applicants. You're given a fat packet of information: lots of tables, data, and text about a business situation. "Read it," they tell you, "then work as a team to answer the five questions at the end. Write up a short report and decide which of you is going to make the presentation. You have thirty minutes. We'll be watching."

It's another impossible assignment, fairly typical of real-life consulting. It tests your ability to work in a team. Can you lead the group in a direction you believe is important? Equally, can you take direction from your peers? During this exercise, avoid being domineering or a wallflower. If you can, display a sense of humor. Listen carefully to your teammates and build on what they say, rather than turning discussions into your own ideas. In these exercises, teams are judged as one, doing well or poorly together. There are no individual winners.

Conclusions

Consulting firms are hungry for talent, which is great news for job seekers. But major firms remain very choosy and applicants can expect to sweat during the interview process. The interviewer's goal is to find out if you have smarts and if you'll interact well with clients. It's your job to prepare in advance for the tricky techniques interviewers use to separate posers from performers.

SELF TEST: IS CONSULTING FOR YOU?

Take this quiz to see how well you're cut out for the consulting life.

Questions
1. When you read *The Wall Street Journal*, your favorite section is:
    a. Money and Investing
    b. Marketplace
    c. Personal Finance
    d. I don't like any parts of *The Wall Street Journal*.

2. Imagine you're a professional athlete. You can pick any sport. Which one fits your temperament best?
    a. Track
    b. Crew
    c. Basketball
    d. Football

3. Your mix of academic performance and social activity at college was:
    a. Top 1% academics, no life.
    b. Top 10% academics, party between assignments.
    c. Top 33%, great social life.
    d. Put it this way: I focused on fun at college.

4. How are you with numbers?
    a. I love pure math, complex numbers, and theorems.
    b. Statistics are pretty cool.
    c. Gimme a calculator and I manage.
    d. I'm a people-person more than a quant-jock.

5. Driving in a strange city, you realize you're lost. Which of the following best describes your reaction?
    a. "Let's find a gas station and ask the attendant."
    b. "The sun's over there, so that must be west, so we should head up here."
    c. "I knew it. We're never going to be on time now. Why didn't you bring a map?"
    d. "Let's keep going until we see some sign or reach the edge of town."

6. What is your attitude toward work and money?
    a. I want to be a millionaire when I'm 30.
    b. I want a job where the work is difficult but I make a lot.
    c. Colleagues, what I'm doing, quality of life - money's lower down the list.
    d. I want to get paid fairly based on what I contribute to my company.

7. Which statement matches your views about work and travel?
    a. I love the idea of seeing lots of different places through my job.
    b. You go where you have to. You make the best of it. No sweat.
    c. It's a necessary evil. You do it when you have to.
    d. Fine as long as I have some control, so I can schedule my life.

8. Favorite types of magazines?
    a. *Fast Company, Fortune, Business Week.*
    b. *Sports Illustrated, Golf, Outside.*
    c. *Time, Newsweek, The Economist.*
    d. Yawn. I don't have time for magazines.

9. What is your attitude on formal business attire?
    a. It's a drag. I prefer casual.
    b. I love it. I want to get hand-tailored suits, expensive shoes, and fashionable ties.
    c. It makes me look older and more credible.
    d. I feel uncomfortable and self-conscious in it.

10. You have to make a toast at a wedding. How do you handle it?
    a. Wing it, but it goes over OK.
    b. Craft detailed speech, practice thoroughly, and deliver it word for word.
    c. Develop outline, ad lib plenty, have guests rolling in the aisles.
    d. Try to get out of it, drink heavily, blush, stammer, get sympathetic applause.

SELF TEST: IS CONSULTING FOR YOU?

Answers

Question	Response	Points	Insight
1.	a.	2	Try investment banking.
	b.	5	Consultants grab the company and business news.
	c.	2	Consultants don't have time to manage their money.
	d.	0	You need to have a genuine interest in business, economics, and finance.
2.	a.	1	Too much a solo activity.
	b.	5	Teamwork, accuracy, stamina, hard work, early mornings sounds a lot like consulting.
	c.	2	Teamwork, but somewhat free-form and unstructured.
	d.	2	Specialized, structured, strategic, considered, but brute force more important than smarts.
3.	a.	2	Congratulations, but consulting firms don't have many back-office career tracks.
	b.	5	Smarts, interpersonal skills and outside interests, just what they're looking for.
	c.	3	If you can get through their tough case interviews, you'll do fine.
	d.	0	Good consultants are very smart and put work first. Call 'em geeks, but there it is.
4.	a.	2	Consider a PhD or risk-arbitrage on Wall Street.
	b.	5	Consultants love opinion polls, regression analysis, and stacked bar charts.
	c.	1	It's hard to avoid number crunching.
	d.	0	You'd be a fish out of water. Consultants are closer to Mr. Spock than Dear Abby.
5.	a.	3	Sensible and practical, but wimps out of solving the problem yourself.
	b.	5	May be wrong, but a good attempt at logical problem solving.
	c.	0	Pessimistic and vindictive. Unpopular on consulting teams.
	d.	0	Indecisive, doomed to failure.

Question	Response	Points	Insight
6.	a.	1	Unlikely. Start an Internet firm or go to Wall Street.
	b.	5	Appropriate expectations for consulting.
	c.	3	Money's often higher on consultants' private lists, but these other factors are vital.
	d.	2	Ain't gonna happen. Try sales and work on a fixed commission percentage.
7.	a.	3	Glad you love travel, but how about seeing the same Holiday Inn 52 weeks in a row?
	b.	5	This is the seasoned consultant's attitude.
	c.	1	Are you a candidate for early burn-out?
	d.	2	Ain't gonna happen, at least not for a few years. Your control is limited.
8.	a.	5	What consultants pick up when they buy magazines at the airport, especially *Fast Company*.
	b.	2	Dream on!
	c.	3	You may be better off in government or journalism.
	d.	0	Sorry, but consultants devour magazines. (If you read biographies of leaders, you get 2 points. Some great consultants we know prefer bios.)
9.	a.	1	Head to Silicon Valley instead.
	b.	2	You may do better in a job where you'll be judged more by the appearance of success than the depth of your intellect. Consultants, as road warriors, tend to be more practical than fashionable.
	c.	5	It may be sad, but it's true.
	d.	0	Feeling like this, you're not going to have fun in consulting, whatever you're wearing.
10.	a.	2	A missed opportunity to shine onstage, and no good for clients.
	b.	3	Solid job, but probably dull and unmemorable, uncompelling for clients.
	c.	5	Notes give you structure, ad libs make you compelling, clients love you!
	d.	0	Trust us, consulting isn't your bag.

SELF TEST: IS CONSULTING FOR YOU?

Interpreting Your Score

Score	Insight
41–50	You are a natural consultant. Don't even think about any other career.
31–40	Consulting may well be for you, but think hard about what makes you tick before joining up.
21–30	We see your future elsewhere, unless you're just signing on for a quick tour of duty.
20 or less	What are you doing with this book?

Interpreting Each Consulting Firm Profile

The following 25 profiles all follow a similar structure, jam-packed with vital information so you can figure out the real differences among the firms. Here's how to make quick sense of all the information:

- ▶ **At A Glance** — shows you how big the firm is, where the headquarters are, who's running the show, who's in charge of recruiting, and how to contact them.
- ▶ **Professional Breakdown** — how many professionals, how many women, how many minorities, how many partners (when available). Gives you a sense of the mix of your future colleagues and the firm's management group.
- ▶ **About The Firm** — start here for a quick introduction to what each firm is about. (When founded, capsule history, any big issues you should know about.)
- ▶ **Services** — what sort of consulting they do.
- ▶ **Career Paths** — all the job titles from entry level to corner office, and how long it typically takes to get there.
- ▶ **Training** — how much there is, when you get it, and what recent hires think about how effective it is. Note: most consultants say that at least 90% of the training is learned on the job, not in the classroom.
- ▶ **Summer Program** — want an internship? Details on the firm's program, including how many interns get a full-time job offer, and how many of them accept.
- ▶ **Recruiting** — which schools the firm targets and what their pitch is like.
- ▶ **Compensation** — typical entry-level salaries for MBAs and BAs, plus signing bonuses. Note: starting salaries don't vary all that much from firm to firm. Most recruits go for the best fit, not the top dollar.
- ▶ **Office Life** — what it's like to work there, in consultants' own words. The good, the bad, and the ugly. Also lists office locations.
- ▶ **Firm Evaluations** — hundreds of MBAs evaluated all the major firms for Kennedy Information. Here's how each firm ranked on prestige, compensation, long-term career opportunities, and quality of life. Plus, quick-fire comments on the firm's culture, what consultants like about the place, and what they hate. Get a sense of whether you'd fit in there.
- ▶ **Leadership Notes** — factoids about the firm's top guns.
- ▶ **Conclusion** — starting advice from recently hired consultants on how to succeed at the firm.

Most consulting firms voluntarily report their financial and other operating data to Kennedy Information. Our analysts review the numbers to make sure that they are consistent from firm to firm. For example, does KPMG define strategy consulting revenues in the same manner as Andersen Consulting? This means that the information presented here includes some numbers as provided to us by the firms and other numbers that are KI estimates.

The quotes from newly-recruited consultants and students are as reported to us in surveys and interviews. KI gets this information from over 1,500 survey respondents each year. We look for consistent patterns and then present the most insightful comments.

Bear in mind that any one comment may reflect all kinds of situations. A harsh criticism could be partly due to the person in question failing as a consultant and then blaming his consulting firm. Another consultant might feel the training he or she received was weak, while not appreciating that it was better than at many other firms. We do our best to avoid presenting isolated accusations from disgruntled people, but we also seek to offer a variety of honest opinions about each firm.

In the end, no firm in these profiles is inherently "better" or "worse" than another. Rather, it may be better or worse *for you*. Use these profiles as a starting point for arriving at your own conclusions.

As many veteran consultants would say, "This is just data. Let's take a look at it and then make up our own minds."

Profiles of 25 Leading Consulting Firms

AMERICAN MANAGEMENT SYSTEMS

at a glance

Year Founded:	1970
Headquarters:	Fairfax, VA
1998 Consulting Revenues:	$913 million
Key Players:	Pat Gross, Vice Chairman
	Frank Nicolai, Executive Vice President
	Paul A. Brands, Chief Executive Officer
	Fred Foreman, Executive Vice President
Number of Consultants:	7,398
Web Page:	www.amsinc.com
Recruiting Contact:	Allan Jones, Manager, College Recruiting
	AMS Inc., 4050 Legato Road
	Fairfax, VA 22033
Phone, Fax, E-mail:	Ph: 703-267-5084, Fx: 703-267-8555
	E-mail: ams_recruiting@mail.amsinc.com

About the Firm

American Management Systems (AMS) was founded in 1970 and has grown each year since. Approximately 90% of its business comes from repeat clients, an indicator of effective work. AMS isn't quite a household name yet, but is probably on its way to becoming one: the firm has a good reputation and positive exposure as one of the 100 best places to work by magazines such as *Fortune* and *Working Mother*. AMS has an emphasis on the US market (hence the name), but is expanding internationally. Approximately 20% of revenues are generated outside of the US, and the firm has 55 offices worldwide. AMS is publicly traded (NASDAQ: AMSY).

Services

AMS provides information technology and operations consulting. It offers more than 30 "productized" services, such as "accounts payable solutions," "Internet service launch," and "emerging technology consulting." Its industry focuses are telecommunications, government, and financial services. Its research and development organization, the AMS Center for Advanced Technologies, is widely recognized as a state-of-the-art laboratory. AMS also has five "Knowledge Centers" focused on the following areas: 1) Business Process Renewal, 2) Systems Development and Information Technology Management, 3) Organization Development and Change Management, 4) Decision Analytics, and 5) Client Relationship and Project Management.

Career Paths

There are no established career paths at AMS, and "if you do your work, it doesn't take very long to get higher up." The loose career path and lack of any up-or-out mentality "works out satisfactorily," say recent hires. MBAs are typically placed in positions of responsibility early on, including stints as team leaders and project managers. New hires begin their work at AMS in one of the firm's vertical market practices (business units). Moving from one business unit to another is possible.

Training

AMS uses a combination of formal courses, self-study, and on-the-job learning with assigned mentors for training.

Summer Program

Summer interns work side-by-side with full-time AMSers on projects. The program begins with much of the same training full-time hires receive, even a presentation on proper dining etiquette. "I definitely needed that one," says one intern. Being part of the team is "real cool" and the firm wants to "make sure that everyone is involved and delivers what they are supposed to deliver." Said one intern: "If I decide to go into consulting, I'd come back here." The interns can learn about all AMS business units and get a feel for the firm culture and environment.

Recruiting

AMS has an on-campus presence at approximately 200 schools across the country and hires from most of them.

Number of Employees Hired 1998–1999

	1998–1999 Season	Expected (*1999–2000 season*)	Summer Associates* (*hired–1999*)
BA/BS	615	625	30
MBA	95	100	8
MS/MPA/Other	125	125	5

*Approximately 85 summer interns were hired for 1998, 70% undergrad and 30% grad
Source: AMS and Kennedy Information/Consultants News

Compensation

Compensation packages for college hires are composed of salary, starting bonuses, and moving and relocation expenses. Benefits include a Dependent Care Spending Account, Employee Assistance Program, Adoption Assistance, Emergency Child Care Services, LifeBalance Program, and the Partners In Employee Relations (PIER) Program. Salary ranges depend on the skills and experiences that new hires bring to the firm plus variables such as educational accomplishments and geographic location. For the 1997-1998 recruiting season, AMS' salaries to new college hires rose by approximately 7% for undergraduates and 8% for MBAs. The firm said signing bonuses were used more frequently in the 1998 season than in the past, varying significantly depending on the degree, skills, and work experience. The talent crunch and stronger student demands have likely forced the increased use of signing bonuses.

Salary Data

	Average Starting Base Salary (1999)	Avg. Signing Bonus (1999)
MBA	$65,000	$12,500

Source: AMS and Kennedy Information Research Group

Office Life

The culture of the firm is "very loose, open, and relaxed" and employees feel free to "go to anyone you need to talk to if you run into a problem." It is a "horizontal hierarchy," if there is such a thing, and the dress code at the Birmingham office (as with most AMS offices) is business casual, which is "really, really nice." Someone who "wants to wear a suit and tie every day isn't going to enjoy it as much." AMS is an "enjoyable" place to work.

Interns have "the same expectations as any permanent employee" in terms of performance and working hours. Traditional ups and downs are normal and "depend on the needs of the client." It also isn't wise to "do your forty hours and then leave" because "everyone works together to accomplish the same goal."

Geographic Locations

Major US Offices	Major Non-US Offices
Atlanta, GA	Bern, Switzerland
Birmingham, AL	Brussels, Belgium
Boston, MA	Dusseldorf, Germany
Charlotte, NC	Frankfurt, Germany
Chicago, IL	Leeds, UK
Denver, CO	Lisbon, Portugal
Fairfax, VA	London, UK
Los Angeles, CA	Madrid, Spain
Minneapolis, MN	Montreal, Canada
New York City	Ottawa, Canada
Redwood City, CA	Slough, UK
Roseland, NJ	The Hague, The Netherlands
Sacramento, CA	Toronto, Canada
San Diego, CA	Warsaw, Poland
Sarasota, FL	

What Don't They Like?

Not having enough notice when you are allocated to another project was one complaint, but if you are unhappy in a project, "they definitely won't say 'tough luck.'" An intern thought management could be "a little more organized," but admitted "I don't really have anything to complain about." All in all, "when people are standing around the coffee machine, they're not fussing about AMS; they're fussing about something outside of work."

Firm Evaluations

MBA Perceptions of AMS (*1-5 scale; 1=poor, 5=outstanding*)

	Prestige/ Reputation	Compensation	Long-Term Career Opportunities	Quality of Life
1999 Rating	**	**	***	*****

Source: Kennedy Information Research Group's 1999 MBA Recruiting Study

Comments from MBA students about AMS

Culture:	Likes:	Dislikes:
"Teamwork, constant learning"	"High responsibility, diverse work"	"Too techie!"
"Collegial, flexible"	"Responsibility quickly"	"Disorganized"
"Decentralized, team-oriented"	"Atmosphere"	"Too technical/ implementation oriented"
"Collegial, friendly, informal"	"Teamwork"	"Little support/training"
"Task-oriented, but starting to focus on people"	"Challenging work"	"Too unstructured, relatively low pay"
"Entrepreneurial"	"Lifestyle"	"Pay, lack of mentors"
"Unstructured, collegial, entrepreneurial"	"Flexibility, manageable lifestyle"	"Business unit mentality"
"Casual, unorganized"	"Flexibility in projects"	"Doesn't retain experienced people"
"Result-oriented"	"Individual responsibility"	
"Fun"	"Opportunity for growth (individual)"	

Leadership Notes

Paul A. Brands, chairman and CEO of AMS, has been with the firm since 1977. Before AMS, Brands spent three years at the Environmental Protection Agency's office of Planning and Evaluation as deputy assistant administrator. Patrick W. Gross, chairman of the AMS Executive Committee, was one of the five founders of the firm in 1970. Frank A. Nicolai, executive vice president and chief administrative officer, is also one of the founders of the firm. Fred L. Forman, in addition to being an executive vice president, is the general manager of AMS' European operations.

Conclusion

Question: If there were any advice that you would give to a new hire or summer associate going into American Management Systems, what would it be?

"Don't judge everything by your first assignment. I formed a lot of opinions when I first got in. It takes a good seven months to find out what's up."
— 20-year-old female intern

"Take as much initiative to learn and get as much out of it as you can, and don't get frustrated. You often start with other new hires. Coming out of college, your head might be spinning. In the beginning of projects, things might be disorganized. Ask questions! They want you to ask. They don't expect you to know anything when you start. Go from there."
— 23-year-old female consultant

"Be open to ideas, willing to learn, be ready for a challenge. We're going to challenge you and push you to do the best work that you can. We're going to help you when you get stuck, but we expect you to be able to pull your way and learn quickly."
— 26-year-old male consultant

ANDERSEN CONSULTING

at a glance

Year Founded:	1989
Headquarters:	Chicago, IL
1998 Consulting Revenues:	$6.720 billion
Key Players:	Joe W. Forehand, Managing Partner
Number of Consultants:	53,416
Web Page:	www.ac.com
Recruiting Contact:	A list of recruiting offices (and there are a lot!) can be found on its Web site on the "careers" tab.

Partner & Professional Breakdown (for consulting activities only)

# Partners	1,251
# Women Partners	N/A
# Minority Partners	N/A
# Professionals	53,416

Source: Andersen Consulting and Kennedy Information/Consultants News

About the Firm

Andersen Consulting (AC) spun off of Arthur Andersen as a separate business unit in 1989 under the Andersen Worldwide umbrella, which wanted to grab a piece of the consulting pie. George Shaheen was named AC's first managing partner, but recently left the position to become CEO of online grocer Webvan. (The new CEO is Joe Forehand.) At its launch, the firm had 21,000 employees and had first-year revenues totaling $1.6 billion.

Along with McKinsey & Company, AC shares the strongest global brand recognition of any consulting firm. Aggressive marketing efforts have yielded impressive results, considering the firm was weaned from Arthur Andersen only 10 years ago. AC began sponsoring professional golf events in 1994, and has continued to improve its brand recognition with innovative marketing, such as sponsoring the Van Gogh exhibit in Washington, DC in 1998.

In late 1997, the firm announced it wanted a divorce from Arthur Andersen (AA) — in an effort to seek independence. As yet, arbitration for the separation (over payment terms and issues such as rights to use the valuable "Andersen" brand name) has not been settled, but Shaheen said AC's growth is "virtually unaffected by the arbitration process." The arbitration is expected to be settled in early 2000.

Services

AC has particular strength in information technology and operations management consulting. Its roots are in large-scale systems-building. The firm serves most industry segments and is strong in manufacturing (35% of total consulting revenues), financial services (25%), telecommunications (15%), and government (10%). The firm develops in its consultants skills in four competencies: Strategic Services (e.g., business strategy), Change Management (e.g., workforce performance improvement), Process (e.g., redesign of business processes), and Technology (e.g., computer systems integration).

AC has successfully augmented service lines to include strategic consulting and outsourcing services in recent years.

Approximately 50% of AC's business is in the US, 35% in Europe, and 10% in Asia/Pacific — a common split for most large global firms with a US base. AC has over 150 offices worldwide.

Major research and development investments (consistently an impressive 5% of revenues) result in new idea generation and effective packaging. AC's St. Charles, Illinois, training facility (which it shares with sister firm AA) is considered the firm's key differentiator, allowing AC to train thousands of consultants each year on common methodologies.

Career Paths

AC defines the rungs of its corporate ladder as follows:

- **Analyst:** Develop core competency skills; eventually, individuals with relevant experience begin to supervise and train others.

- **Consultant:** Strengthen supervisory skills; develop solid foundation in application of core competency and problem-analysis skills.

- **Manager:** Broaden team management skills; expand skills in specific competency; become expert in industry or other specialized areas.

- **Associate Partner:** Deepen specialized skills in business, industry, and competency areas; exercise thought leadership in client projects; expand entrepreneurial skills.

- **Partner:** Supervise client relationships; forge new and enduring client relationships; exercise independent judgment in business development; become a leader in professional and civic communities.

AC offers several career options that cater to individual preferences. A consultant can sample the different competencies, stick with one he or she likes, or move across industry sectors. In Strategic Services, undergraduate hires spend three to four years as business analysts and then typically return to business school.

A consultant usually gets formal feedback at least twice a year, as well as regular informal feedback. Salary reviews and adjustments come annually. Promotions are based on strong job performance, demonstrated proficiency in the required skills, and firm needs. Career paths generally lead to the associate partner position or possibly to the partner position if the consultant is a "best performer."

Training

In addition to on-the-job learning, AC provides a formal training program, and puts its money where its mouth is. In 1997 alone, the firm spent an impressive $430 million on training. Offerings depend on previous experience, career level, client responsibilities, and career track. The firm has training centers around the world, the largest of which is the Center for Professional Education in St. Charles, Illinois.

All new recruits go through an orientation program in their local office, part of which is standardized. New AC employees take "New Employee Orientation," a CD-ROM course that helps them get acquainted with the firm. Other parts of orientation are customized for that particular local office or geographic area. AC also provides training for employees based on ability.

Change Management new hires participate in the Human Performance Design School. New hires learn to solve the performance problems of major financial services companies. Their role is that of an analyst for this simulated engagement, based on an actual AC project. The experience will build their skills in instructional design, graphical user interface design, usability testing, communication planning, issue analysis, client interaction, and performance assessment.

Consultants have described the St. Charles learning center as "a wonderful place to meet new people and learn about the company." Overall, the training is "very, very good" and considered "expansive and allows you to meet the real partners at the firm." A consultant who had several years of consulting experience said "in terms of training, I would bet AC is one of the best."

Summer Program

AC is selective about choosing interns — intern candidates go through the same screening and interview process as recruits who are pursuing full-time positions. Interns are expected to perform meaningful work on client projects, often on-site. In addition, the firm runs several programs for interns, including a summer intern conference that nearly every intern attends.

Interns are expected to "perform as if they were new analysts" but "without the six weeks of training." Client contact "depends on the assignment, and the role you are playing." Another expectation is to "take advantage of every opportunity that may arise." Intern lifestyle isn't bad because they are "pampered by the recruiters and on projects." But they are expected to "push themselves to attain new skills" and be "professional and timely." One intern said he "was not given any training as a summer intern" because "we were expected to have some type of technical background whether it was computers or a form of engineering."

Recruiting

AC recruits at many of the major schools, and the firm was listed as one of the three top hirers in *Business Week's* B-school ranking issue. According to Kennedy Information Research Group, given AC's size, over 8,000 consultants a year leave AC for various reasons, so recruiting simply to replace the consultants AC loses is aggressive and "taken very seriously." "Sooner or later, every employee either volunteers or is called on to participate" in recruiting efforts. The firm, however, isn't driving herd; students say that the interview questions are "more in-depth than at the average firms" and "the interview style is one of the toughest." Three rounds of interviews prune prospective recruits.

Recruiting schedules include information sessions, career fairs, awards banquets, events (lunches, dinners, mixers, receptions, barbeques with giveaways), and in-office visits. Some of the questions address "the way you think and the thought processes you may have gone through in carrying out a particular task," including a series of scenario questions for which you need to tell of a personal experience. The process itself is described by both consultants and interns as "excellent." Some like that "if you ask the right questions, they will give 100% straight answers."

Number of Employees Hired 1998–1999

	Actual* (*academic yr. ending: 6/1999*)
BA/BS	6,200
MBA	1,200
MA/PhD/Other Students	800
Industry Experts	9,300

*All figures are approximate and are global figures. US figures are approximately one half of the global figures.
Source: Andersen Consulting and Kennedy Information/Consultants News

Compensation

At AC, compensation is competitive with the other industry giants. New MBAs joining in 1998 from top 5 schools received $99,600 base salaries plus signing bonuses. Perks are "ongoing" and sometimes tied to individual projects, but can include a car and apartment (when staffed out of town). One intern liked that AC provided him relocation expense reimbursement. An experienced consultant said "the longer you stay with the firm, the happier you become with your individual compensation package."

Benefits include 401(k)/profit-sharing plans, health care, salary continuation for vacation and illness, long-term disability insurance, life insurance, and an employee assistance program (EAP). The EAP is provided to help employees with work/life and other personal issues.

Office Life

People "work hard and play hard" at AC. The culture is "very young" and has a "college-like atmosphere," but AC has a reputation for long hours, and the lifestyle of an AC consultant is "more for individuals without lots of ties to an area." One intern observed "your project is your family" when you work at AC. The same individual is "not saying you can't have a life outside of Andersen Consulting, but when you are on the road all week away from your family, it becomes tiring." It is also essential to "remember you are judged by the quality of your work" and also "how well you can deal with the people above you and below you." Hours at all levels differ depending on the client work, and new hires can expect to work regular hours as much of their time is spent on internal training. All consultants and partners usually face longer hours when project deadlines approach.

Since many people come and go due to traveling or new projects, camaraderie "may not always be that easy." The firm has done "a fine job" of promoting teams and teamwork in order to promote solidarity. "I know I have never been afraid to ask a question of anyone on my team," said one intern. "Everyone is willing to help answer a question or share an Andersen Consulting experience." On many of the teams and "because we all come to understand what we do and how different it is from the mainstream, we automatically develop a strong sense of camaraderie." When individuals meet others who work at the firm, "they already feel like they have so much in common."

Geographic Locations
US Offices

Albany, NY	Irving, TX	Phoenix, AZ
Atlanta, GA	Jackson, MS	Pittsburgh, PA
Austin, TX	Kansas City, MO	Portland, OR
Baton Rouge, LA	Las Colinas, TX	Raleigh, NC
Boston, MA	Los Angeles, CA	Richmond, VA
Charlotte, NC	McLean, VA	Sacramento, CA
Chicago, IL	Memphis, TN	St. Louis, MO
Cincinnati, OH	Miami, FL	St. Petersburg, FL
Cleveland, OH	Milwaukee, WI	San Diego, CA
Columbus, OH	Minneapolis, MN	San Francisco, CA
Dallas, TX	Nashville, TN	San Ramon, CA
Denver, CO	New York, NY	Seattle, WA
Detroit, MI	Northbrook, IL	Springfield, IL
Florham Park, NJ	Oklahoma City, OK	Tallahassee, FL
Hartford, CT	Orange County, CA	Tampa, FL
Houston, TX	Palo Alto, CA	Walnut Creek, CA
Indianapolis, IN	Philadelphia, PA	Washington, DC

Non-US Offices

Amsterdam, The Netherlands
Athens, Greece
Auckland, New Zealand
Bangkok, Thailand
Barcelona, Spain
Beijing, China
Berlin, Germany
Bilbao, Spain
Bogota, Colombia
Bombay, India
Bratislava, Czech Republic
Brisbane, Australia
Brussels, Belgium
Budapest, Hungary
Buenos Aires, Argentina
Canberra, Australia
Cape Town, South Africa
Copenhagen, Denmark
Dublin, Ireland
Dubai, United Arab Emirates
Dusseldorf, Germany
Etobicoke, Canada
Frankfurt, Germany
Hamburg, Germany
Helsinki, Finland
Hong Kong, China
Jakarta, Indonesia
Jeddah, Saudi Arabia
Johannesburg, South Africa
Kuala Lumpur, Malaysia
Lagos, Nigeria
Lisbon, Portugal
London, UK
Luxembourg
Lyon, France
Madrid, Spain
Manchester, UK
Manila, The Philippines
Melbourne, Australia
Mexico City, Mexico
Milan, Italy
Monterrey, Mexico
Montreal, Canada
Moscow, Russia
Munich, Germany
Nagoya, Japan
New Delhi, India
Newcastle, UK
Osaka, Japan
Oslo, Norway
Ottawa, Canada
Paris, France
Porto, Portugal
Prague, Czech Republic
Pretoria, South Africa
Rio de Janeiro, Brazil
Riyadh, Saudi Arabia
Rome, Italy
San Juan, Puerto Rico
Sao Paulo, Brazil
Seoul, South Korea
Sevilla, Spain
Shanghai, China
Singapore
Sophia Antipolis, France
Stavanger, Norway
Stockholm, Sweden
Sydney, Australia
Taipei, Taiwan
Tokyo, Japan
Toronto, Canada
Turin, Italy
Valencia, Spain
Vancouver, Canada
Verona, Italy
Vienna, Austria
Vigo, Spain
Vitoria, Spain
Warsaw, Poland
Wellington, New Zealand
Windsor, UK
Zaragoza, Spain
Zeist, The Netherlands
Zurich, Switzerland

ANDERSEN CONSULTING

Is This Firm for You?

AC is for "anyone who likes a challenge and can deal well with change. The challenge comes from the constant need to learn and apply new things." Another important attribute is to be able to budget your time well, because if you don't "you will get burnt out very quickly." Maintaining a balance "is the key and if you can't do that it will be a big problem." Taking the initiative to "speak up for the things you personally want to do" is another desired quality in order to work at AC. It goes without saying that you also have to be acquainted with the consultant lifestyle and be able to live with it.

What Don't They Like?

While AC received high scores in KI's MBA survey on "prestige" and "compensation," the firm scored poorly in terms of "quality of life." That the firm ranked #55 out of 59 firms in 1997 and #50 out of 52 firms in 1998 says a lot about its perceived lifestyle. Several MBAs who had worked at AC before B-school were unhappy with the long hours, travel requirements, and the career track, which is "elongating and increasingly tenure-based." The firm is also not immune to other complaints. One consultant has gripes about a "do-it-as-it-has-been-done methodology," while another complained the firm "could do a better job with our staffing process. There are times where there will be a number of unstaffed individuals buzzing around the office." But the firm is attempting to make "collective down time" more valuable. Retention is another Achilles heel: AC "needs to focus more on retaining its good people." Due to the size of the firm and the huge number of people it recruits, "it is difficult to cater to everyone's needs." However, AC "is becoming more aware of why people stay or leave, and is working towards better retention."

Firm Evaluations

MBA Perceptions of Andersen Consulting (*1-5 scale; 1=poor, 5=outstanding*)

	Prestige/ Reputation	Compensation	Long-Term Career Opportunities	Quality of Life
1999 Rating	*****	****	****	*

Source: Kennedy Information Research Group's 1999 MBA Recruiting Study

Comments from MBA students about Andersen Consulting

Culture:	Likes:	Dislikes:
"Team-oriented"	"Progression, training"	"Structured style"
"High speed"	"Friendly"	"Bureaucratic"
"Diversity"	"Vast knowledge capital"	"Long career path"
"Successful"	"Resources, size"	"Size"
"Global"	"Diversity"	"Slow policy changes"
"Tech-oriented"	"Flexibility, long-term opportunity"	"Technical side"
"Learning culture"		"Perceived IT-centered image"
"Young, energetic"	"The excitement, variety"	"Too long to make partner"
"Open, relaxed"	"Great exposure"	"Tight schedules, lack of quality"
"Dynamic, fast-paced"	"Candid relationship with clients"	
"Knowledge powerhouse"		"Long hours"
"Goal-oriented"	"Clear career path, early responsibility positions"	"Disorganized administration"
	"Talented, cooperative teammates"	

Leadership Notes

George Shaheen, former managing partner and CEO, had guided AC from its birth in 1989 to September of 1999, when he resigned his position to become CEO of Internet grocer Webvan. Shaheen joined Andersen Worldwide in 1967 and became a partner in 1977. Before his appointment as managing partner of AC, he was managing partner of of the Southeast US Region and North American practices, as well as the practice director for Japan and the Pacific Northwest. He was replaced November 1, 1999 by Joe W. Forehand, a 27-year veteran of Andersen. Highly qualified, Forehand held leadership positions in 11 of the 16 industries served by the firm since becoming a partner in 1982.

Conclusion

Question: If there were any advice you could give to a new hire or summer associate going into Andersen Consulting, what would it be?

"Understand fully what you are becoming a part of. Make sure that you are the type of person who has a zest for learning and can handle responsibility."
— consultant in the Technology Competency and Communications Industry practice

"Take the opportunity to learn about the firm from the inside, networking and asking as many questions as possible. If a summer associate returns to Andersen Consulting as a new hire, networking can provide opportunities to work on specific

projects the new hire may be particularly interested in. They should also be proactive and pursue as much responsibility as they can."
— summer intern in the Technology Competency practice

"Seek out information and ask a lot of questions. Become friends with the people in your start group. Network with everyone that you meet."
— summer intern in the Process Competency practice

"Go in with an open mind, ask lots of questions (of course, at the appropriate times), watch people, and listen."
— summer intern in the Process Competency practice

"Make sure you take full advantage of every opportunity within the firm. There are various opportunities where one can learn a skill as well as speak with partners and managers about the firm itself. Always be willing to learn, be patient, and ask questions."
— summer intern in the Technology Competency practice

AON CONSULTING

at a glance

Year Founded:	1994 and 1995
Headquarters:	Chicago, IL
1998 Revenues:	$615 million
Key Players:	Patrick Ryan, Chairman and CEO of Aon Corporation
	Donald Ingram, Chairman, Aon Consulting, Inc.
	Daniel Cox, Chairman, Aon Consulting Worldwide
Number of Consultants:	4,100
Web Page:	www.aonconsulting.com
Recruiting Contact:	Joanne Meyer
Address:	123 North Wacker Dr., Suite 1100
	Chicago, IL 60606
Phone, Fax:	Ph: 312-701-2339, Fx: 312-701-4960

About the Firm

Aon Consulting is a half-billion dollar division of Aon Corporation, which provides risk management and reinsurance services, and insurance underwriting. Aon Consulting was formerly known as Godwins International. In December 1996, Aon acquired Alexander & Alexander Services, which doubled its revenues. The firm is known for its *U.S. Risk Management Survey* and a similar survey in the UK; Aon-line, which offers risk managers online access to Aon professionals; and the publications *Alert* and *Forum,* which keep Aon clients updated on developments in compensation, change management, and employee benefits and HR. The firm has 38 offices in Europe (28 in the United Kingdom), 19 in the United States, 11 in Canada, and 9 in Asia/Pacific.

Services

Aon Consulting serves most industries and chiefly provides human resources consulting (approximately 75% in benefits and compensation). It also has a growing HR outsourcing practice. Aon is strong in the financial services, healthcare, and manufacturing industries. Its services are grouped into four buckets: 1) Human Resources, 2) Employee Benefits, 3) Compensation, and 4) Change Management.

Career Paths

There are several roads that lead to the consultant level at the firm, though there's not a whole lot of "structured training." One consultant was not aware of a minimum training requirement at the firm, with outside and inside training "encouraged but not required." If you are interested in more education, they'll "send you anywhere you want to go." All you have to do is "say the words," and they'll let you take a course. One consultant said that after one day of orientation he began work the next day. Regardless, the orientation and training are "pretty effective" and "give you the information you want to find out."

Summer Program

The firm does not have a summer program, nor is there a formalized intern program.

Recruiting

Aon is not very active or well-known on college campuses. As a result, MBAs polled in KI's recruiting study ranked Aon relatively low. The firm "primarily gets people through word of mouth," and because of the firm's standing in insurance brokerage and underwriting, it "recruits from insurance carriers." One Aon consultant mentioned "we don't recruit a lot at college campuses." In her case, she just heard "a lot of good things about Aon" at another company she was with. After visiting the firm, she found that Aon had "a lot of career potential."

On-Campus Recruiting

Schools from which the firm actively recruits
Catawba
Elon
Gilford
High Point University
Meredith College
University of North Carolina at Chapel Hill
University of North Carolina at Greensboro
Wake Forest

Source: Aon Consulting and Kennedy Information/Consultants News

Compensation

Compensation at Aon is "good — not great, but fair." Another person was told during her interview that "you're not going to make as much money here, but you won't work those kinds of [long] hours." It seems "when you're happy with your job and the people, money isn't as much of an issue." Employee benefits include health, dental, vision, 401(k), life insurance, and accidental death and dismemberment coverage.

Office Life

An Aon consultant might work "forty or forty-five" hours a week, a little more "depending on the season" if you're in employee benefits consulting. August to November is the "busy season," but the only real expectation is "when projects are hard, you work late." To keep hours reasonable, they "provide lots of support staff." There are "several levels to distribute the work." There is "a lot of flexibility," such as working at home. Travel is fairly minimal because most clients are local to Aon offices. People who choose can be issued a modem to use at home to "hook right into the network" at the Aon office.

There's a "very good spirit of cooperation" at the firm and "people get along very well." One consultant "kept wondering if people were going to show their true colors," but no one ever did. Summer hours are "pretty easy going," and the atmosphere in general is "a great environment to work in." There are frequent social functions during and after business hours, and the firm "decorates the office for Halloween." (No one, however, dresses in costumes.)

Most Aon consultants highly recommend their firm as a great place to work. The only thing mentioned as something the firm could improve upon was lack of training on "internal protocols." A "little more structure" is how another consultant put it. One consultant mentioned that "as big a corporation as this is, I never feel lost in the numbers."

Geographic Locations

US Locations

Atlanta, GA	Fairfax, VA	Parsippany, NJ
Baltimore, MD	Grand Rapids, MI	Pittsburgh, PA
Boston, MA	Grosse Pointe Farms, MI	Portland, OR
Briarcliff Manor, NY	Horsham, PA	Raleigh, NC
Cedar Rapids, IA	Houston, TX	San Francisco, CA
Charlotte, NC	Jacksonville, FL	Santa Fe, NM
Chesterfield, MO	Los Angeles, CA	Seattle, WA
Chicago, IL	Lyndhurst, NJ	St. Louis, MO
Columbus, OH	Mercerville, NJ	Tampa, FL
Conshohocken, PA	Minneapolis, MN	Washington, DC
Coral Gables, FL	New York, NY	Winston-Salem, NC
Detroit, MI	Newport Beach, CA	
Eden Prarie, MN	Norwalk, CT	

Non-US Locations

Aberdeen, UK	Brussels, Belgium	Glasgow, UK
Adelaide, Australia	Calgary, Canada	Harrogate, UK
Amsterdam, The Netherlands	Cardiff, UK	Harrow, UK
	Cornwall, UK	Leeds, UK
Antwerp, Belgium	Croydon, UK	London, UK
Auckland, New Zealand	Dublin, Ireland	Madrid, Spain
Birmingham, UK	Edinburgh, UK	Manchester, UK
Brisbane, Australia	Edmonton, Canada	Melbourne, Australia
Bristol, UK	Farnborough, UK	Milan, Italy

Non-US Locations (continued)

Montreal, Canada	Sheffield, UK	Toronto, Canada
Moscow, Russia	Singapore	Vancouver, Canada
Newcasle, UK	Southampton, UK	Vilnius, Lithuania
Nottingham, UK	St. Albans, UK	Wellington, New Zealand
Paris, France	Stockholm, Sweden	Woking, UK
Regina, Canada	Sydney, Australia	Zurich, Switzerland
Saskatoon, Canada	Thunder Bay, Canada	

Leadership Notes

Patrick G. Ryan, president and CEO of Aon Corporation, has held that position since 1982 (but the firm wasn't named Aon Corporation until 1987). Daniel T. Cox, chairman of Aon Consulting Worldwide, has been with the firm since 1986, when he was called upon to develop Aon's benefits consulting practice. Prior to joining Aon, Cox was managing director of William M. Mercer–Medinger, Inc. Donald C. Ingram, chairman of Aon Consulting, was president and CEO of actuarial employee benefits consulting firm Brooke & Company, which merged into Aon in 1993.

Conclusion

Question: If there were any advice you could give to a new consultant going into Aon Consulting, what would it be?

"Never be afraid to ask questions, because it clarifies a lot of things. Don't let things snowball. I think management has always been very open discussing questions and concerns. Even questions about benefits. I've been extremely happy with my job."
— 29-year-old female associate

"Don't be afraid to ask questions. The people here are very willing to help and lend a hand."
— 29-year-old female benefits consultant

ARTHUR ANDERSEN

at a glance

Year Founded:	1913
Headquarters:	Chicago, IL
1998 Consulting Revenues*:	$1.368 billion
Key Players:	Jim Wadia, Worldwide Managing Partner
	Richard Boulton, Managing Partner, Strategy & Planning
	Chuck Ketteman, Managing Director, Business Consulting
Number of Consultants:	9,196
Web Page:	www.arthurandersen.com
Interested Recruits:	Call AA's corporate headquarters, or get on its web site for the nearest of its 363 worldwide offices

*Includes revenues in the Strategy, Finance, and Economics Practices

About the Firm

The firm was founded by Mr. Arthur Andersen in 1913, and has a widely recognized brand name — being one of the sibling companies of Andersen Worldwide, a $10+ billion dollar professional services organization. Arthur Andersen (AA) has 363 offices in 78 countries, but only started pursuing the consulting biz in 1992, three years after watching sister company Andersen Consulting (AC) grow explosively. Last year, AA's audit/tax services still represented a larger chunk of revenue than its consulting business, but the consulting side is growing faster. The growth is attributed to its brand name and aggressive marketing campaign, which made AC bristle, saying AA is invading AC's turf. Nonetheless, marketing efforts continue in major business publications, and while the arbitration matter is still under discussion, AA is prospering.

Services

The firm provides primarily operations management and information technology services. AA claims to focus on the middle market — defined as organizations with $200 million to $2 billion in revenues — so as not to overlap with AC, though former AC Worldwide Managing Partner George Shaheen says the firm has encroached on "our space." Approximately 40% of its consulting revenues are generated inside the United States. AA's "KnowledgeSpace," an online business Q&A service (akin to Ernst & Young's "Ernie"), and its "Global Best Practices" databases are aggressively marketed.

Career Paths

New BA recruits join as consultants and remain at that level for up to five years. Promotion, according to AA officials, "depends on business need, experience, and performance." The levels beyond consultant are manager, senior manager, principal, director, and partner. Recruits comment that if you're on the "fast track" you can "get up the ladder and make partner in 12 years," which one consultant thought was "incredible." "Outstanding performance" enables consultants to exceed the normal speed of career progression. Consultants can move from one practice area to another and to other offices. Instead of an "up or out" mentality, the firm describes its career paths as a "grow or out" approach.

MBA hires may join the firm as a manager or be promoted to one within three years, depending on performance. Beyond the manager level, MBAs have the same career steps as other employees. Like undergrads, their paths may be faster, contingent on performance and business need. After consultants have developed expertise in a particular practice area, they begin to take a role in Market Facing Teams, which are industry — or business solution — focused.

Training

The firm provides over 1,000 hours of in-house training for new consultants. Consultants new to the organization and the profession attend a "New Consultant Program," which incorporates considerable technology training. New hires with experience in consulting or business attend a program called "The Way We Consult," which focuses on the "tools of the trade" and shows consultants what methodologies and resources AA has to offer. The firm also boasts a Center for Professional Education in St. Charles, Illinois. According to the firm, 69,000 people participate in training and meeting activities at the facility each year. Consultants seem to like their "big training budget" and the fact that they get to "meet people from all over the world" during the training sessions. The firm has "a requirement of 80 hours of training a year," and the focus of training can be "whatever you want."

Summer Program

AA's summer program "varies from office to office," but interns typically begin with a short orientation program before joining a project team. The initial training may be "minimal," but interns are able to attend seminars on topics such as mentoring and team building. Summer associates are "treated like full-time consultants" and put in "about 50 hours a week." The only real expectation was to "come in and work on assignments" and the firm does a "pretty good job on the program considering the time constraints."

Summer Associate Data

Percent of 1998 BA/BS summer associates who were offered full-time positions:	41%
Percent of offers made that were accepted:	74%
Percent of 1998 MBA summer associates who were offered full-time positions:	81%
Percent of offers made that were accepted:	59%

Source: Arthur Andersen and Kennedy Information/Consultants News

Recruiting

AA claims to be the first professional service firm to have recruited on college campuses. Today, it recruits widely at 140 schools. During its presentation, you "feel like they care about you" and you learn about the culture, which is "down to earth and likable."

Number of Employees Hired 1998–1999 (US)

	Actual (*academic yr. ending: 6/1999*)	Expected (*academic yr. ending: 6/2000*)	Summer Associates (*hired – 1999*)
BA/BS	871	1000	176
MBA	92	105	21
MA/PhD/other students	69	80	3

Source: Arthur Andersen and Kennedy Information/Consultants News

On Campus Recruiting (selected schools):

	# of BA/BS recruits (FY98)		# of MBA recruits (FY98)	
Schools	*Interviewed* *	*Hired*	*Interviewed*	*Hired*
Arizona State University	29	18	8	3
Baylor University	18	12	4	3
Boston University – Graduate School	NA	NA	12	4
College of William & Mary	22	10	1	0
Emory	7	2	15	2
Georgetown	15	4	1	0
Miami University – Ohio	27	15	0	0
Texas A&M University	36	14	4	1
University of Arizona	41	25	12	2
University of California at Los Angeles	39	21	0	0
University of Illinois	49	11	2	0
University of Maryland	15	8	2	1
University of Notre Dame	62	18	0	0
University of Southern California	23	11	7	2
University of Texas at Austin	50	18	12	2
University of Virginia	47	10	0	0

* The number interviewed includes only campus recruits who were invited for an office visit.
Source: Arthur Andersen and Kennedy Information/Consultants News

Compensation

Compensation for new consultants is "above average," and one summer associate described the compensation of about $3,500 a month as "very nice." Consultant compensation can range significantly. According to one consultant, the firm is "really good about keeping our salaries above the market level." All new recruits are eligible to make 401(k) contributions. Benefits include interest-free transition loans to new hires as well as paid moving expenses and various discounts. CPA and some other professional exam fees are reimbursed. Depending on the level at which recruits are hired, they may be eligible for promotion bonuses, profit sharing, and gain sharing.

Salary Data

	Avg. Starting Base Salary ('99)
BA/BS	$42,631
MBA	$55,897
Other	$47,066

Source: Arthur Andersen and Kennedy Information/Consultants News

Office Life

According to our interviews, there is a great deal of meritocracy at AA, and "no one wears titles on their sleeves." The culture is "very comforting" and "young," with a work hard/play hard mentality. Other than holiday parties, there is a summer gathering consultants informally call a "field day" that includes sporting events and "just fun stuff." People are comfortable with "asking for a day off for personal reasons" as long as their client demands are met. A consultant said "it's all about the people and the culture here," and the firm is "very careful" to hire people who will be a good fit. Headhunters call, sometimes offering "twice the money," but many consultants "wouldn't do it because the culture is so great."

One recruit commented that when consultants first join the firm, they "don't have a lot of control" as far as the number of work hours is concerned. As you get to know people in staffing and the managers who run the projects, "you can influence what projects you're put on," but some project assignments depend on luck and what is going on. When a project hits crunch time, "you are expected to put in nights and weekends," but that is the exception. However, if you took a job at AA and thought you'd never work a night or weekend, "you'd be out of your mind."

You can get "lots of face time with CFOs and CIOs." AA is recommended for anyone "who wants to get a broad experience." One consultant said he had been on fifteen projects in two years "in a lot of different industries with a lot of different clients."

Geographic Locations

US Locations	# Professionals	Non-US Locations	# Professionals
Atlanta, GA	675	United Kingdom	498
Chicago, IL	326	Spain	270
Houston, TX	320	Latin America	260
Los Angeles, CA	243	Japan	251
New York, NY	231	France	205
San Francisco, CA	199	Germany	168
Dallas, TX	172	Italy	159

Source: Arthur Andersen and Kennedy Information/Consultants News

Firm Evaluations

MBA Perceptions of Arthur Andersen (*1-5 scale; 1=poor, 5=outstanding*)

	Prestige/ Reputation	Compensation	Long-Term Career Opportunities	Quality of Life
1999 Rating	***	***	**	*

Source: Kennedy Information Research Group's 1999 MBA Recruiting Study

Comments From MBA Students About Arthur Andersen

Culture:	Likes:	Dislikes:
"Tight"	"Support and mentoring"	"Size"
"Business advisors"	"Friendships with co-workers"	"Unfocused, no strategy, lack of vision"
"Hierarchies"	"Training"	"Face time"
"Team-oriented"	"Range of available assignments"	"Lack of creativity"
"Sophisticated, yet informal"	"Responsibility, growth"	"Managing culture/mindset"
"Client-oriented, dedicated"	"Industry exposure"	
"Young, social, intelligent"		
"Exclusive, emphasis on documentation"		
"Multidisciplinary"		

Source: Kennedy Information's 1999 MBA Recruiting Study

What Don't They Like?

Some at AA feel there "could always be more money." AA is making "more of an effort with the bonus programs, which they haven't done in the past" and "one thing they could improve upon is an evaluations system that pinpoints performance a little better." Most other complaints from AA recruits were directed more towards consulting in general than AA specifically.

Leadership Notes

Richard Boulton, the managing partner of the strategy and planning practice, was appointed in September of 1997, when he was 38 years old. Jim Wadia was appointed to his post as worldwide managing partner in July 1997, succeeding Richard Measelle. Wadia, like AC's George Shaheen, made a bid a few months earlier to become the CEO and managing partner of Andersen Worldwide and failed to get the votes needed to obtain that position.

Conclusion

Question: If there were any advice you would give to a new hire or summer associate about to join Arthur Andersen, what would your advice be?

"I would say the most important thing is to find out who you enjoy working with, who you work with well, and work with those people. To get on the projects you like, work with these people. In the end it comes down to your relationships."
— 24-year-old male consultant

"Because of the nature of our business, AA is very entrepreneurial, so you have to come in and want to manage your career. If you want technology, you can get it —you just need to ask for it. If you sit around and wait for it to happen, it won't happen."
— 23-year-old male consultant

"Ask lots of questions. If you ever feel uncomfortable, ask. You'll be surprised how many people are willing to give you an answer."
— 21-year-old female summer intern

ARTHUR D. LITTLE

at a glance

Year Founded:	1886
Headquarters:	Cambridge, MA
1998 Consulting Revenues:	$608 million
Key Players:	Lorenzo Lamadrid, president, CEO
	Tom Sommerlatte, Chairman, Management Consulting
Number of Consultants:	2,141
Web Page:	www.arthurdlittle.com
Recruiting Contact (US and Canada):	North America Recruitment Coordinator
	Arthur D. Little
	Acorn Park
	Cambridge, MA 02140-2390
Phone, Fax:	Ph: 617-498-6070, Fx: 617-498-7140
Recruiting E-mail:	careers@adlittle.com

About the Firm

Arthur D. Little (ADL) is the world's oldest consultancy — the firm was founded in 1886 and has a long-standing reputation as a technology-based strategic consulting firm. The firm has 14 offices in North America, and over 40 offices elsewhere. ADL has a well-known commitment to training at its A.D. Little School of Management, which has trained over 3,000 employees from 117 countries since its birth in 1964.

Arthur D. Little Enterprises (ADLE) is a collection of companies that nurture and guide technologies from infancy through final applications in the high-tech, industrial, medical, and consumer industries. Over half a billion dollars worth of products are sold worldwide under licenses from ADLE. The firm often brags — and rightfully so — about its assignments with new technological developments. A recent project was to "validate the capabilities" of a "brew basket decaffeinator" that removes the caffeine from coffee after it has been brewed.

The firm took a hit in early 1999 when Charles Lamantia was allegedly forced into stepping down as CEO when European partners, dissatisfied with ADL's recent performance, threatened they'd walk. Lorenzo Lamadrid has since replaced Lamantia. The firm has experienced lower than average growth over the past few years (e.g. approximately 3% in 1998), but with its new leadership anticipates that growth will accelerate.

Services

ADL offers services in eight areas: 1) Strategy, 2) Organization, 3) Information Management, 4) Operations Management, 5) Technology and Innovation Management, 6) Technology Creation and Exploitation, 7) Design and Development, and 8) Environment, Health, and Safety. ADL's roots are in science and technology, but the firm serves a variety of industries: automotive, chemicals, consumer goods, energy, financial services, medical products, metals and resources, pharmaceuticals, the public sector, TIME (telecom, information, media and electronics), transportation, travel, tourism and hospitality, and utilities.

Career Paths

Undergraduates join the firm as analysts and are put on a case right away. Analysts stay in their position at the firm for two or three years, then return to graduate school, but not necessarily to obtain an MBA. ADL offers scholarship programs for students who have "demonstrated their abilities on case work." MBAs join the firm as consultants and later become manager, senior manager, associate director, and director. In the director's chair they are responsible for new business development and strengthening client relationships. Typically, it takes "seven years to become 'partner,'" and one consultant thought it was "absolutely" a reasonable path.

Training

The firm has "a formal week of training for people each time they enter a new career stage," and more senior staff "tend to get more training in things like administration, managing people and larger client assignments, and sales." The initial training session involves the teaching of ADL methodologies, and is "pretty good." The session did have a "mix of analysts and consultants" and the only significant complaint was that someone wished the firm "gave us more time to get to know the people around us."

Summer Program

ADL has a formal summer program geared toward first-year MBAs. The firm says the program, in addition to being an "exciting experience," also acts as a "qualifying period for consultants." The firm says that "many" interns are invited back to the firm after they complete their graduate programs. Interns act as consultants on case teams and are trained in ADL's "methodologies, models, and approaches."

Recruiting

ADL actively recruits at the schools listed below, but "accepts resumes from a much broader range of schools." The firm "probably hires more people from outside of MBA schools" than do most of its competitors, and senior staff at ADL "tend to be from industry." There is "less reliance" on the MBA hiring circuit than at many other firms. The "ability to show that you are curious and have industry knowledge" carries more weight than your actual degree.

Number of Employees Hired 1998–1999

	Expected (*academic yr. ending: 6/1999*)	**Summer Associates** (*hired–1998*)
BA/BS	40–60	N/A
MBA	70–80	20–25
MA/PhD/ and Other Industry Experts	150–200	N/A

Source: A.D. Little and Kennedy Information/Consultants News

On-Campus Recruiting

Schools from which the firm actively recruits
Cornell
Harvard
IESE
IMD
INSEAD
Michigan
MIT (Sloan)
Northwestern (Kellogg)
Princeton
University of Chicago
University of Pennsylvania (Wharton)

Source: A.D. Little and Kennedy Information/Consultants News

Compensation

Entry-level compensation is comparable to that at other large firms. ADL "places a great deal of importance" on total compensation, especially given that "all employees obtain company stock." One consultant thought it was a "drawback" that too much of the compensation (even the 401(k) money) is tied to company stock, perhaps because the stock's value hasn't been keeping up with Wall Street recently. One analyst felt that short-term compensation is "below that of other major consulting firms, but steps are being taken to address this."

Salary Data

	Average Starting Base Salary (1998)	**Avg. Signing Bonus (1999)**
BA/BS	$48,000	$6,000
MBA	$95,000	$25,000

Source: A.D. Little and Kennedy Information/Consultants News

Office Life

The Cambridge facility has been described as "cinderblock hell" by one consultant, who said that the design "represents the fact that many of the offices were converted laboratories." But you do get an office — not a cubicle — regardless of your level. This facility "encourages you to get out of the office and get to the client site, which isn't bad for business." The other offices in the United States are more ordinary, and the San Francisco office is "the nicest" with its "complete view of the Golden Gate Bridge."

ADL has a "professional, curious, and innovative" culture, and it tends to attract people who like challenging work. "Many have PhD's," and ADL people in general are "very smart." The consultants "seem to enjoy each other's company" and "the senior staff are very willing to take the time to work with the junior people."

Partners and consultants work between fifty and seventy hours a week. If you "stayed late or came in on a weekend, people would certainly be there," but consultants "make considerable efforts" to manage their work and personal life. People who have a "scientific bent" will tend to be happier at ADL, but "if you're naturally curious and are willing to work hard, the firm can be a place of unlimited opportunities."

Geographic Locations

US Offices	Non-US Offices	
Arlington, VA	Abu Dhabi, United Arab Emirates	Milan/Rome, Italy
Cambridge, MA		Moscow, Russia
Chicago, IL	Bogota, Colombia	Paris, France
Houston, TX	Brussels, Belgium	Prague, Czech Republic
Irvine, CA	Buenos Aires, Argentina	Riyadh, Saudi Arabia
North Charleston, SC	Cambridge, UK (CCL)	Rotterdam, The Netherlands
Palo Alto, CA	Caracas, Venezuela	Sao Paolo, Brazil
Philadelphia, PA	Dusseldorf, Germany	Seoul, Korea
San Francisco, CA	Hong Kong, China	Singapore
Santa Barbara, CA	Kuala Lumpur, Malaysia	Stockholm, Sweden
Seattle, WA	Lisbon, Portugal	Sydney, Australia
Waltham, MA	London, UK	Thornhill, Ontario, Canada
Washington, DC	Mexico City/Monterrey, Mexico	Tokyo, Japan
	Madrid, Spain	Vienna, Austria
	Melbourne, Australia	Zurich, Switzerland

What Don't They Like?

One consultant said the company needed to improve on ADL's general level of "mass market awareness," because some people "think ADL is an accounting firm, which it's not." Another said that the innovative culture and people's desire to have "a large degree of autonomy" over their work makes it "particularly hard to develop the core methodologies that are familiar to people at other firms." The firm is "currently making progress" in this area.

Firm Evaluations

MBA Perceptions of Arthur D. Little (*1-5 scale; 1=poor, 5=outstanding*)

	Prestige/ Reputation	Compensation	Long-Term Career Opportunities	Quality of Life
1999 Rating	***	****	****	***

Source: Kennedy Information Research Group's 1999 MBA Recruiting Study

Leadership Notes

Lorenzo Lamadrid was formerly the president of Western Resources International until he came on board as president and CEO of A.D. Little in July 1999. Lamadrid ended Charles Lamantia's 11-year reign as leader of A.D. Little, who resigned in late 1998 in response to disgruntled partners and sluggish growth. It remains to be seen whether Lamadrid has the right stuff to push the firm into double digit growth once again.

Conclusion

Question: If there were any advice you would give to a new hire or summer associate going into A.D. Little, what would it be?

"The faster you can build industry depth, the greater responsibility you will have."
— 28-year-old male consultant

"I think the people who do very well here are people who are proactive and seek out creating their own network. Getting involved is probably the best advice I could give someone, and if you're coming out of school, take that summer off before starting."
— 28-year-old female consultant

"I would say get exposed to as much as possible in the firm with respect to its capabilities and its knowledge base. ADL has a lot to offer, so approach people. I'd add also that senior management listens and is responsive to associates' needs and ideas with how to improve the practice."
— 31 year-old-male consultant

A.T. KEARNEY

at a glance

Year Founded:	1926
Headquarters:	Chicago, IL
1998 Consulting Revenues:	$1.23 billion
Key Players:	Fred Steingraber, CEO
Number of Consultants:	2,880
Web Page:	www.atkearney.com
Recruiting Contact:	Robert Chrisner, Dir. of Human Resources
Address:	222 W. Adams St., Chicago, IL 60201
Phone, Fax:	Ph: 312-223-6025, Fx: 312-223-7548

Partner & Professional Breakdown (for consulting activities in North America only)

# Partners	114
# Women Partners	9
# Minority Partners	12
# Professionals	725
# Women Professionals (excluding partners)	146
# Minority Professionals (excluding partners)	169

Source: A.T. Kearney and Kennedy Information/Consultants News

About the Firm

A.T. Kearney (ATK), founded by Andrew Thomas Kearney in 1926, has operated under the A.T. Kearney name since 1946. The firm is one of the older management consulting organizations and is strong in strategy and operations management. In 1995, the firm was acquired by Electronic Data Systems (EDS), an IT firm founded in 1962 by Ross Perot.

The ATK name is recognized worldwide, and to date, EDS appears to have no plans to fold the name into the EDS umbrella, such as what happened to CSC Index (which was blended into its Computer Sciences Corporation parent). Despite industry-wide skepticism that ATK could thrive under EDS control, the firm has performed well and negatives have been minimal (EDS did downsize a hefty amount of its employees in mid 1999, and ATK laid off some non-billable individuals).

ATK also has an executive recruiting division, A.T. Kearney Executive Search, which is the 11th largest retained search firm in the U.S., according to *Executive Recruiter News*.

Services

In addition to operations and strategy work, ATK offers information technology services in its three divisions: 1) Products and Services; 2) Relationships with Customers, Suppliers, Shareholders, Partners, and Employees; and 3) Economics through Revenue and Productivity Gains. Revenues from IT consulting have reportedly risen faster than revenues from strategy or operations services for the last few years, and ATK is emerging as a significant player in e-commerce consulting.

Career Paths

Undergraduates start as analysts and usually remain there for three years, after which they typically go to back to school to get an MBA. MBA hires start as associates and can expect to become managers after about two years. The manager will become a principal after two or three years, and later a vice president. All consultants are generalists.

Training

For new hires there is a week of firm orientation and another week of what is described as "effective" training, which includes basic report writing, speaking, and presentation skills. ATK has a series of training classes that last one to four days; consultants at all levels take — on average — three or four sessions each year.

Summer Program

There is a ten-week summer program with a three-day orientation before setting to work on a client or internal project. One intern remarked how he "joined on a Monday, flew to the office where the partner was working, read up on what he had done so far on the project, and was at the client site on Thursday." Suffice it to say, anyone who likes to be "briefed in the air" would enjoy the ATK program.

Recruiting

ATK recruits from several of the top-tier business schools and recruits about half as many undergraduates as it does graduates. The firm has a "well-put-together presentation" and sells students on where the firm will be in five years and how they can be a part of it. The presentation itself is "fairly similar" to other firms', but ATK "uses more technology in its presentation."

Number of Employees Hired 1998–1999

	Actual (*academic yr. ending: 6/1999*)	**Expected** (*academic yr. ending: 6/2000*)	**Summer Associates** (*hired 1999*)
BA/BS	33	80	13
MBA	136	115	50
MA/PhD/Other Students	7	8	N/A

Source: A.T. Kearney and Kennedy Information/Consultants News

On-Campus Recruiting

Schools from which the firm actively recruits

Columbia
Northwestern
Princeton
Stanford
Texas
University of Chicago
University of Pennsylvania

Source: A.T. Kearney and Kennedy Information/Consultants News

Compensation

Compensation is "not super competitive," but competitive with the industry. One manager at the firm says the compensation at his level ranges from $110K to $150K. Summer associates who accept job offers can get tuition reimbursement. If you are consistent and "keep doing good work," you can expect rewards.

Salary Data

	Average Starting Base Salary (1999)	Avg. Signing Bonus (1999)
BA/BS	$47,500	$5,000
MBA	$95,000	$25,000

Source: A.T. Kearney and Kennedy Information/Consultants News

Office Life

One source thinks the firm "flat out expects" sixty hours a week, with an average of three to four days a week of traveling. When there are a lot of hours, there can be "a lot of drinking together" and dinners out. The consultants "try to avoid weekends," though some projects stretch to 80-hour weeks at crunch time. Work and life can be "relatively balanced," and one person noted that the partners work "about the same hours as everyone else."

The firm has a "down to earth" culture and everyone "seems committed to each other." You are given "a lot of freedom to do what you want" and the partners and managers help "shape your future in the firm." The firm has a "very progressive" maternity leave program and also accommodates special needs of individual consultants. One PhD who looked at McKinsey and BCG said culture was the determining factor when he selected ATK.

Individuals who would like the firm would probably be "pragmatic, results-oriented people" who consider themselves to be interpersonally "adept and flexible." Consultants who apply to ATK should be "approachable and fairly secure with themselves." Another happy consultant would recommend the firm to "absolutely anyone."

Geographic Locations

Major US Offices	Major Non-US Offices
Atlanta, GA	Berlin, Germany
Cambridge, MA	Hong Kong
Chicago, IL	London, UK
Costa Mesa, CA	Tokyo, Japan
Dallas, TX	
New York, NY	
San Francisco, CA	
Washington, DC	

What Don't They Like?

Like any firm, ATK has some challenges, and there are "a series of things we always work on improving." Campus recruiting could be "stronger." In general, people are encouraged to speak up about problems. One complained the firm "isn't doing as much intellectual work as we should" and there should be more "thought leadership." As if responding to this command, ATK recently came out with a thought leadership journal called "Executive Agenda," and is underwriting a public television series called "CEO Exchange," which was launched in January 2000.

Firm Evaluations

MBA Perceptions of A.T. Kearney (*1-5 scale; 1=poor, 5=outstanding*)

	Prestige/ Reputation	Compensation	Long-Term Career Opportunities	Quality of Life
1999 Rating	*****	*****	*****	***

Source: Kennedy Information Research Group's 1999 MBA Recruiting Study

Comments from MBA Students About A.T. Kearney

Culture:	Likes:	Dislikes:
"Friendly, helpful, supportive"	"Accessible senior partners"	"Bureaucracy"
"Relaxed, down-to-earth"	"Knowledgeable co-workers"	"Long projects"
"Midwest, sincere, conservative"	"Allow for significant responsibility, growth"	"Capturing of intellectual capital"
"Bureaucratic, suits"	"Clients they have"	"Monday to Friday travel"
"Collegiate"	"Very practical, results-oriented"	"Diversity"
"Strong work ethic"	"Complete range of projects"	
"Pragmatic, hands-on"	"Smart, fun, down to earth people"	

Leadership Notes

Fred G. Steingraber became CEO in 1983 and has been with ATK for over a third of a century. Before his appointment as CEO, Steingraber was elected Chief Operating Officer (COO). Since he became CEO, ATK's revenues have approximately doubled every three years. Prior to Steingraber, the firm was led by Kenneth L. Block, who retired in 1985.

Conclusion

Question: If there were any advice you would give to a new hire or a summer associate going into A.T. Kearney, what would it be?

"Take advantage of the firm's open culture by seeking out the people that you think you'll want to work with, look to as a mentor, or learn from in other ways. I'd also tell people to practice immediately putting yourself in the shoes of our clients to understand their needs and how they want to interact with consultants. And frame for themselves what they want from their career at Kearney so that they can navigate their way to finding it."

— 32-year-old male full-time consultant

"Make sure you don't get lost in the shuffle, because the firm is getting big. Also get to know people and latch onto projects or proposal efforts."

— 35-year-old male manager

"Be yourself. Make sure that you be true to whatever you're doing. They give you a lot and expect a lot. As long as you perform, you'll do all right."

— 27-year-old male summer associate

BAIN & COMPANY

at a glance

Year Founded:	1973
Headquarters:	Boston, MA
1998 Consulting Revenues:	$564 million
Key Players:	Thomas Tierney, Worldwide Managing Partner
	Orit Gadiesh, Chairperson
Number of Consultants:	1,650
Web Page:	www.bain.com
Recruiting Contacts:	Jennifer Fulton (Undergraduates)
	Crisolita Pontes-Ives (MBA)
Address:	2 Copley Place, Boston, MA 02116
Phone, Fax:	Ph: 617-572-3163, Fx: 617-572-2427

About the Firm

"Bain! We're gonna live forever!" So went the song (parodying the popular TV show "Fame") as sung by "Bainies" at their holiday parties back in the 1980s, when the young firm was leapfrogging giddily toward the head of the pack of top-tier strategy firms. It almost didn't happen.

Founded by ambitious maverick Bill Bain, who dramatically spun the firm off of BCG in 1973, Bain grew bigger than its more staid parent through a sharp focus on implementing the strategies it designed (common brochure babble nowadays, but Bain was a pioneer). Disaster struck in 1989, when a brutal combination of recession, overly ambitious expansion, a very expensive financial restructuring (to buy back the shares of founder Bill Bain), the loss of key rainmakers, and peripheral involvement as consultant to brewer Guinness (which took over rival Distillers — themselves advised by Bain spinoff LEK — amid cries of stock manipulation) all led Bain almost to implode.

A slimmed-down Bain, with new management, subsequently rose from the ashes and then resumed its march toward becoming one of the top strategy firms in the business. More so than arch-rivals McKinsey and BCG, Bain tends to view the consulting "profession" as a "business." Esoteric strategy is fine, but the point is to get the client's share price up. To that end, Bain promotes itself with an index that shows how the stock prices of its clients have steadily outperformed the market. Not surprisingly, Bain also has a large and very successful venture capital group, run largely independently from the consulting firm. With its aggressive style, Bain is one of the truly entrepreneurial large consulting firms. (Starting a company is one of the more popular reasons consultants leave.)

Services

Bain is a strategy specialist that most often deals with CEOs at the top of the corporate ladders at *Fortune* 1000 companies. New consultants won't spend much time with CEOs. However, implementing strategies involves heavy face time with middle managers. Corporate strategy, business unit strategy, organizational strategy, sales and marketing strategy/loyalty, mergers and acquisitions/privatization, and distribution and logistics are among Bain's offerings. The firm also provides venture capital/investment services through its subsidiary, Bain Capital, which is literally across the hall from the consulting division at its Boston headquarters.

The firm has 11 European offices, 5 US offices, and 4 Asia/Pacific offices. Almost 50% of revenues are generated outside of the US. It serves most industries (see list) and has individual specialists, not firmwide practice areas. Bain is particularly strong in financial services, manufacturing, and media/communications. It is becoming increasingly aggressive in product development and branding concepts (e.g., *The Loyalty Effect,* by Bain consultant Fredrick R. Reichfield).

Practice Area Breakdown

Note: There are no formal assignments to practice areas
- Automotive
- Consumer Products
- Financial Services
- Growth
- Health Care
- Information Technology
- Loyalty
- Mergers & Acquisitions
- Private Equity
- Reengineering
- Telecom & Technology

Career Paths

Undergraduate hires typically work for two to three years prior to attending business school, while MBA hires usually work as consultants for three to four years and then are promoted to managers. The march to vice president usually takes another three to four years, after which you are made partner.

Training

New recruits participate in a week-long, off-site, team-based training program. There are additional training programs at each major career point (experienced consultant training, case team leader training, manager training, and vice president training). These programs are supplemented by an on-line, interactive training system. At the beginning of their careers, consultants are assigned to two cases simultaneously, which the firm claims allows them to gain exposure quickly to different industries and business issues.

Summer Program

Summer interns are assigned to a client case team for the 10-week program. Work streams are structured to provide interns with a discrete assignment they can own, with a clear end point. The summer program also includes a formal training session and a number of social events to acquaint interns with as many potential colleagues as possible. Bain says "the majority of our summer interns do receive offers for full-time employment."

Summer associates (SAs) seem pleased with the program. Client contact varies from project to project, and expectations are high, but don't feel unattainable. "We are expected to deliver," said one summer associate. "You can't just goof off. You also have review processes. Your work stream is important and is measured by tangible output." Another says, "[summer associates are] expected to display analytical and strong team skills and the ability to add value." The same SA was satisfied with client contact. "My specific experience here has been good client contact, yet not overwhelming client contact. The situation gives me time to focus on the client as well as internal things at Bain." Another more experienced consultant who originally was in the summer program said it is one of Bain's strongest attributes. "They put a lot of emphasis on the summer program. I had partners ask me to dinner and lunch, and just talk to me to make sure all the questions I had got answered."

Recruiting

Bain recruits mainly from top-tier US business schools. Whenever possible, alumni recruit at their alma maters. "Their presentation was great," said one consultant. "It had a lot of energy. That was my first impression of Bain: it was a hard-working firm to be at." Another mentioned that Worldwide Managing Director Tom Tierney was effective at introducing the firm to the students and is "a very good ambassador for Bain." The firm's efforts pay off; it has a great "win rate" among candidates who get an offer, second only to McKinsey's.

Number of Employees Hired 1998–1999

	Actual (*academic yr. ending: 6/1998*)	**Summer** *Associates* (*hired–1998*)
BA/BS	200	50
MBA	180	95

Source: Bain & Co. and Kennedy Information/Consultants News

Compensation

Bain offers a "competitive compensation package that includes tuition reimbursement and a year-end bonus." Consultants had good things to say about their compensation. One found his signing bonus "considerable" and was offered a relocation package as well. Another full-timer said, "Bain clearly stands out as top-notch" when discussing compensation. The firm also reimburses B-school tuition for people who have worked at Bain beforehand. Summer associates' descriptions of their compensation range from "great" to "similar to the other leading firms."

Office Life

Bain's Boston headquarters was recently renovated. "It's very open, lots of glass, seats are in open areas, and you have access to quiet glassed-in rooms." Headquarters has areas called bays, and there are four to six mini-cubicles in each bay, while the managers and partners have offices. The space is "very open, which is part of the cultural theme" with the consultants in a sharing environment. "You wouldn't walk down the halls of Bain and see mahogany doors, all closed," said one consultant. The bays also allow consultants with different experience levels to sit with one another, which "makes it easy to ask the stupid questions."

Typical workweeks vary by assignment. If the project is demanding, "you're expected to be here as long as it takes." Bainies usually work 50–55 hours overall. "People don't spend all their weekends here. It's not a terrible lifestyle." Another variable is the amount of travel, of which there can be "a lot." (No surprise, given Bain's penchant for heavy client involvement and the fact that Bain has fewer offices than some of its rivals.)

The culture is "a strange mix of laid-back and intense." It's laid-back in the way people communicate with one another. It's intense where "people seem very passionate about what they do." One thing that's great about Bain is that "you're given a lot of responsibility. If you can get your part of the case finished, no one says you have to be here from eight to eight." The general consensus at the firm is that long hours are expected when the task demands, but not otherwise.

Geographic Locations

Major US Offices	Major Non-US Offices		
Atlanta, GA	Beijing, China	Hong Kong	Madrid, Spain
Boston, MA	Brussels, Belgium	London, UK	Rome, Italy
Chicago, IL	Geneva, Switzerland	Moscow, Russia	Toronto, Canada
Dallas, TX	Mexico City, Mexico	Sao Paulo, Brazil	Tokyo, Japan
Los Angeles, CA	Munich, Germany	Seoul, Korea	Sydney, Australia
San Francisco, CA	Paris, France	Singapore	Stockholm, Sweden

What Don't They Like?

When asked what the firm does poorly or could do better, we heard relatively few gripes. However, while the training is strong, some say there isn't a lot of guidance. "You can drive your own work and have your own impact," which means the firm may not be suitable for people who like more structure. The no-nonsense approach Bain has been known for sometimes takes clients aback. "We put the analysis before the client management skills," said one consultant. "There can be some tense moments at a client site. [Bain] will never tell the client what they want to hear, if there is a pet project that the management shouldn't do. Personally, I like it, but some don't."

Firm Evaluations

MBA Perceptions of Bain & Co. (*1-5 scale; 1=poor, 5=outstanding*)

	Prestige/Reputation	Compensation	Long-Term Career Opportunities	Quality of Life
1999 Rating	*****	*****	*****	****

Source: Kennedy Information Research Group's 1999 MBA Recruiting Study

Comments from MBA Students About Bain & Company

Culture:	*Likes:*	*Dislikes:*
"General management"	"Interesting assignment"	"Hours, workload"
"Go getter, 80–20"	"Global opportunities"	"Lack of diversity"
"Enthusiastic, informal"	"Methodologies"	
"Insightful"	"Autonomy"	
"Work hard, play hard"	"Performance-driven"	
"Fact-based"		
"Entreprenuerial"		
"Results-focused"		

Leadership Notes

Prior to Orit Gadiesh's appointment as chairperson, Bain was lead by Mitt Romney, who was the firm's CEO from 1991 to 1993 (he left to continue leading Bain Capital). It can be argued that without Romney, Bain would have collapsed under its immense debt. Recently, Romney was called upon again to save the scandal-plagued Salt Lake City Olympics, temporarily leaving his Bain Capital post to go to the rescue.

Chairperson Orit Gadiesh is from Israel, and served in the Israeli Army while in her teens. While some consultants learn strategy from their high school chess club, Gadiesh probably picked up some valuable lessons working in the Israeli intelligence war room. She's been chairperson since 1993, and is still best friends with Romney, whom she met in 1977 when he was one of the people interviewing her for a job at Bain. She's certainly one of the most prominent women in consulting, and her effective leadership indicates she'll be elected for a third three-year term as chairperson.

Conclusion

Question: If there were any advice you would give to a new hire or summer associate about to enter Bain & Company, what would it be?

"Get to know people at the different levels. There's a tremendous amount of people at Bain who are very open. From a culture standpoint, this is a great place."
— 25-year-old female summer associate

"Take full advantage of your experience and maximize learning every day. The best experience at Bain is when you integrate yourself into the firm — helping out with recruiting, being a trainer, getting yourself involved in the 'extras.' People will find a lot of learning and development opportunities here if they're active."
— 31-year-old male full-time consultant

"Take advantage of the firm's flexibility. Bain is doing a lot on the issue of choice for the employee. If you want to work part-time, it's easy to do. There's flexibility in this firm that you can't ignore."
— 31-year-old male summer associate

"Be as proactive as you can be once you get there. There's so much in regards to the people, resources, and traditions here at Bain. Take the initiative to seek out new things and learn new things."
— 26-year-old female summer associate

"Don't hesitate to use the resources around you. You're gonna have an easier time and a lot more fun when you tap into the network here. People are open and forthcoming in sharing their experiences at Bain. Jump in with both feet the moment you get here."
— 28-year-old female full-time consultant

BOOZ-ALLEN & HAMILTON

at a glance

Year Founded:	1914
Headquarters:	McLean, Virginia
1998 Consulting Revenues:	$1.2 billion
Key Players:	Ralph W. Shrader, Chairman and CEO Daniel C. Lewis, President, Worldwide Commercial Business practice
Number of Consultants:	6,540
Web Page:	www.bah.com

Recruiting Contacts

Graduate Recruiting	Undergraduate Recruiting	Industry Recruiting
Cheryl Muia	Lisa Matkovic	Lillian Pacheco
101 Park Ave.	101 Park Ave.	101 Park Ave.
New York, NY 10178	New York, NY 10178	New York, NY 10178
Ph: NA	Ph: 212-551-6010	Ph: 212-551-6533
Fx: 212-551-6200	Fx: 212-551-6200	Fx: 212-551-6200
E-mail: muia_cheryl@bah.com	E-mail: matkovic_lisa@bah.com	E-mail: pacheco_lillian@bah.com

About the Firm

Booz-Allen & Hamilton (BAH) was founded in 1914 by Northwestern University alum Edwin Booz. The firm has a widely recognized name and an enviable reputation, particularly in government (about 40% of revenues) and manufacturing. BAH is deep in operations management and has been focusing more on technology and implementation in the last few years. Some of its clients include Boeing, Mobil, Deutsche Telekom, San Francisco's municipal transit system, and the IRS (hope they succeed with that one!). Presently, the firm has over 8,000 employees in nearly 100 offices, 62 of which are in the US, 8 in the Asia/Pacific region, 8 in Europe, and 5 in Latin America. BA&H publishes monthly newsletters on communications/media/technology, health/insurance, and banking and capital. In addition, the firm publishes the quarterly management journal, *Strategy & Business*.

Services

In its own words, BAH "adheres to a 'triple crown' philosophy, helping clients in strategy, technology, and operations, unlike our competitors, who focus only on one or two of those areas." The firm serves most industries through seven lines of business: 1) Consumer and Engineered Products, 2) Communications/Media/Technology, 3) Energy/Chemicals and Pharmaceuticals, 4) Financial and Health Services, 5) Information Technology, 6) Operations Management, and 7) Strategic Leadership Practice, which encompasses growth strategies, change management, the role of CEO and top management, and "building strategic capabilities and people strategies."

Career Paths

Undergraduates come into the firm as "consultants." At the entry level, consultants generally work on research and analysis, while more senior consultants assist in strategy development and management of client teams. Usually, consultants spend two to three years at BAH before enrolling in graduate school, often MBA programs. Many are sponsored by the firm and are provided tuition assistance and other support while at school.

MBA hires enter the firm as "associates," which BAH describes as "at the heart of the typical project team." Entry-level associates conduct analysis, client interviews, client team management, and strategy development. Associates with more experience are responsible for strategy module development, presentations, and management of "junior team members." Associates are typically promoted to senior associate in two to three years.

In the US and Europe new hires are placed within one of the seven practice areas. New hires in Asia and Latin America are placed geographically.

Training

New hires, undergraduate or graduate, can expect a six-day new-hire orientation that covers everything from the history of the firm to how to fill out expense reports. Mainly it is "about how Booz does business." Many partners are involved, and the new hires may have half-day sessions on strategy and/or case sessions on operations, for instance. A mock case may be included in the sessions, where recruits work in teams. The training programs are off-site, take place around the world, and when the program is complete, new hires return to their field offices. Many friendships can be built among the new hires, with one consultant "still in e-mail contact with the folks" he met two years earlier. Camaraderie among the "class" is high, but "the real learning is on the job."

Summer Program

Interns and summer associates at BAH are assigned a mentor. The base qualifications the firm looks for in an intern are 30 credit hours of completed course work, a declared major in any field, and a 3.0 GPA. The Worldwide Technology Business (WTB) offers summer and academic-year internships, as well as co-op opportunities.

Recruiting

BAH actively recruits at many top campuses. Its on-campus presentation has "top-notch partners attending," and the firm puts "a lot of effort into it." Though it had "a bunch of information" about BAH and was a "real representation of the firm," it was "pretty much the same" as the presentations of the other consulting firms. One consultant was sold on the firm after he was "wined and dined" and got to know BAH people after the presentation.

Number of Employees Hired 1998–1999

	Actual (*academic yr. ending: 6/1998*)	Expected (*academic yr. ending: 6/1999*)
BA/BS	110+	100+
MBA	250+	250+
MA/PhD/Other Students	50+	50+
Industry Experts	150+	150+

Source: Booz-Allen & Hamilton and Kennedy Information/Consultants News

Schools from which the firm actively recruits

MBAs	Undergraduates
Carnegie Mellon	Columbia University
Columbia	Harvard University
Darden	MIT
Fuqua	Morehouse College
Harvard	Northwestern
INSEAD	Princeton University
Kellogg	Spelman College
University of Michigan	Stanford University
MIT	University of Chicago
Stanford	University of Pennsylvania
University of Chicago	Wellesley College
Wharton	Yale
Yale	

Compensation

Undergraduates can receive a signing bonus, relocation money, and a year-end bonus, in addition to "very competitive" compensation. For one undergrad, the "relocation and signing bonus was $4,000" and his compensation package was in the "high forties." Another liked that he was "at the top end of the range" among his friends who went to leading firms.

MBA compensation can include tuition reimbursement for summer interns and sponsored consultants, a signing bonus, and year-end performance bonus. Employee benefits at all levels include domestic partner benefits, an emergency (or backup) day care center, medical care, paid personal leave, a resource and referral service, flexible work arrangements, medical and dependent care, dispersal accounts, tuition reimbursement, and an employee assistance program.

Salary Data

	Average Starting Base Salary (1998)
BA/BS	$46,000–$55,000
MBA	$80,000–$95,000
MA/PhD/Other Students	$80,000–$95,000

Source: Booz-Allen and Kennedy Information/Consultants News

Office Life

The New York office, which houses about 400 consultants, has "interesting artwork" with "a grand staircase, which goes up through the floors." Associates are "typically in cubes," and offices are often occupied by two consultants, but it is "still a pleasing place to work." People are generally "only in the office on Fridays."

During certain weeks you might work "nine to six," and there are weeks when you could "work nine to eight or nine to nine." There is no single expectation of how many hours you have to work, but it is "more of a question of what the team needs to get done together to get the job done." Usually the weeks "leading up to a deliverable will be hectic." Weekends are sometimes involved, but as a whole, they are "respected," and if "you work Saturday, you don't have to come in Sunday." The real key to balancing your work and life at BAH "is to give them good notice" when a weekend or evening is untouchable. In general, during the week working at the firm "means going back to a hotel" at night.

There are many "different personalities" at the firm, but "anyone interested in consulting would like" working there. One consultant would "recommend it to anyone," especially to people who ultimately want to go into industry because "you get a chance to specialize" at the firm. The ideal BAH consultant is "versatile and doesn't have a problem jumping into problems." It is also recommended that you be a "willing traveler," but nearly "anyone could be happy here."

Geographic Locations

Major US Offices	Major Non-US Offices	
Chicago, IL	Bangkok, Thailand	Milan, Italy
Cleveland, OH	Bogota, Colombia	Mumbai, India
Dallas, TX	Buenos Aires, Argentina	Munich, Germany
Houston, TX	Caracas, Venezuela	Paris, France
Los Angeles, CA	Dusseldorf, Germany	Sao Paulo, Brazil
McLean, VA	Frankfurt, Germany	Seoul, South Korea
New York, NY	Hong Kong	Singapore
San Francisco, CA	Jakarta, Indonesia	Sydney, Australia
	London, UK	Tokyo, Japan
	Mexico City, Mexico	

What Don't They Like?

BAH conducted an employee survey recently and found out what people thought and what grievances they had. For one, there needs to be "a greater attempt to have get-togethers among consultants without a recruiting angle" to it. According to BAH people we spoke with, there are always "some issues all around" but nothing that would deter consultants from staying with the firm. Similar to McKinsey, Booz scored very high in Kennedy Information's survey on every criterion except quality of life.

Firm Evaluations

MBA Perceptions of Booz-Allen & Hamilton (*1-5 scale; 1=poor, 5=outstanding*)

	Prestige/ Reputation	Compensation	Long-Term Career Opportunities	Quality of Life
1999 Rating	★★★★★	★★★★★	★★★★★	★★

Source: Kennedy Information Research Group's 1999 MBA Recruiting Study

Comments from MBA Students about Booz-Allen & Hamilton

Culture:	*Likes:*	*Dislikes:*
"Go get 'em"	"People, diversity"	"Siloing of functions"
"Fact-based, quantitative, analytical"	"Fits people with different styles"	"Operationally focused"
"Professional, intellectual, smart"	"Intellectual challenge"	"Early industry specialization"
"Acronym-driven"	"Challenging projects"	"Frantic work pace"
"Hardworking, intense, demanding"	"Non-political"	
"Self-driven, focused"	"Global opportunities"	

Leadership Notes

William F. Stasior, who has held the position of chairman and CEO since 1991, retired on April 1, 1999. Ralph W. Shrader, who was the leader of the Technology Business Group, succeeded him. Brian Dickie, who had been the president of the Worldwide Commercial Business practice since 1993, resigned unexpectedly in mid-1998 to pursue other interests outside of consulting. BAH was shocked, but quickly named Daniel C. Lewis, formerly managing partner of the firm's global Consumer and Engineered Products group, as Dickie's successor.

Conclusion

Question: If there were one piece of advice that you would give a new hire or a summer associate going into Booz-Allen & Hamilton, what would it be?

"Get to know a lot of people. Especially as a new hire, it's good to have a support [group]. Forming relationships early is very important. Be as proactive as possible, don't be afraid to ask for help; no one expects you to know everything. And enjoy it. Count your lucky stars. Realize the value of the work that you're doing."

— 25-year-old male consultant

"Be prepared to work hard. Come in, work hard, and it's quite a ride. Be prepared for something completely new. Be prepared to make some good friendships and strong relationships. The people here are great, so learn to leverage them. You're (sort of) never alone."

— 23-year-old male full time consultant

BOSTON CONSULTING GROUP

at a glance

Year Founded:	1963
Headquarters:	Boston, MA
1998 Consulting Revenues:	$730 million
Key Players:	John Clarkeson, Chairman
	Carl Stern, President/CEO
Number of Consultants:	1,940
Web Page:	www.bcg.com
Recruiting Contact:	Roxane Cullinan,
	North American Recruiting Manager
Address:	200 S. Wacker Drive
	Chicago, IL 60606
Phone, Fax:	Ph: 312-993-3300, Fx: 312-876-0771

About the Firm

In the same elite class as Bain and McKinsey, Boston Consulting Group (BCG) was founded in 1963 and has remained as one of the top strategy boutiques. The firm has an enviable track record as a "conceptual leader"; BCG developed the buzzwords "time-based competition" and Segment of One marketing. Its *Perspectives* journal is published 10 times per year. Like McKinsey, the firm has a history of working only for the top management at major corporations (who can afford the gargantuan fees). BCG also gave birth (albeit unwillingly) to Bain & Company back in 1973. The firm has a great reputation for compensation, career opportunities, and (amazingly enough) quality of life among MBAs in Kennedy Information's annual survey. The firm has 40 offices around the world, only a quarter of which are in the US.

Services

Individual consultants have industry experience, but BCG doesn't market its consulting based on accumulated industry wisdom. The firm markets its expertise in: branding, consumer goods and retail, corporate development, e-commerce, energy and utilities, financial services, globalization, healthcare, high-tech, industrial goods, IT, operational effectiveness, organization, and pricing.

BCG has long had a reputation for working at the more "conceptual" end of the consulting spectrum. You could well find yourself helping clients answer the question "what business should I be in?," for example. While there will always be a market for "pure advice," this angle is materially different from the more technical approach of a firm like Andersen Consulting.

Career Paths

Undergraduates start off as associates at the firm and will be in that position for one to three years, after which "many" associates return to school for an MBA or another graduate degree. During the first two years as a consultant, the mission is "to acquire and demonstrate a range of skills, including quantitative analysis, interviewing, conceptualizing, writing, working with the client, and teamwork." After another year or so, consultants may qualify to become case leaders, and later a manager. After a total of "six to eight" years at the firm, the patient and hard working few may become officers.

Training

Introductory training is usually a few weeks in duration (called "boot camp" by one consultant) and is "very good for networking and peer group building." Formal training is available for about the first six months of a consultant's career; consultants can pursue additional training if they choose. There is also a mentoring program. The training is "effective" and BCG is always "working on things to make it better." Still, the training that occurs on the job is "the best kind of training they provide." New hires report to learn the most when they are "elbow to elbow with the consultants."

Internship Program

BCG does have an internship program, but it is one of few firms that downplays summer programs on its Web site. However, the firm does have an interesting "Interactive Case Study" on its site, which provides some consultant practice. A case is described and you have 12 hours to solve it. There is a list of questions you can ask the client, similar to a "choose your own adventure" book. At the end you can pick a recommendation and find out how you did and how a BCG case team would have presented the findings. Though obviously not an internship program, the Interactive Case Study does provide practice in the consulting arena.

Recruiting

BCG recruits from top schools around the world. The firm's interview involves "standard interviews with professionals and potential colleagues" in a "very personable" style. BCG gladly accepts cover letters or phone calls from interested students if their particular school isn't one where the firm actively recruits. However, most BCG recruits tend to come from top-ranked schools such as Harvard and Stanford.

Compensation

MBAs ranked BCG second among 50 firms for compensation in both 1998 and 1999, although starting compensation is reported to be "average for the top consulting firms." The firm gives signing bonuses and profit sharing to new MBA hires. A case team leader three years out of business school typically earns around $115K, year-end bonus of $20K, plus profit sharing. At the manager level, pay is "between $130K and $145K." The year-end bonus for a manager can be "between $20K and $50K." The bottom line: BCG is competitive with its peers, and the firm is known to be "distributive," in that profits are dispersed relatively widely among employees.

Office Life

There are "intelligent people and interesting work" at BCG, while there is "kind of a family unit" in project teams. Teams are typically comprised of three consultants, a manager, and an officer, with "a ton of interaction" among them. At the office, consultants at all levels "care a lot about each other," but you "don't feel obligated to spend time together outside of work." One consultant appreciated that you don't have to spend time with people "for political reasons."

Unusual among consulting firms, BCG "doesn't lose a lot of people because of lifestyle." Consultants in Boston "try to get local work." When people do leave the firm, it is often because an industry client will call them with "an offer they can't refuse." Quite a few people leave "to pursue entrepreneurial opportunities."

One consultant in the Boston office remarked that "the place is pretty empty by 7:00 at night" and "they don't turn the air conditioning on during the weekends." (How does he know?) Consultants care more about what they produce as opposed to "how hard you work to produce it." As a manager, you might "put in solid eleven-or twelve- hour days, five days a week," but rarely work weekends. Not a lot of consultants seem to think hours are "out of whack." Of course, during crunch time, you work until it's done. The firmwide philosophy is making the work/life balance "work in the long term."

Geographic Locations

US Offices	Non-US Offices		
Atlanta, GA	Auckland, New Zealand	London, UK	Shanghai, China
Boston, MA	Bangkok, Thailand	Madrid, Spain	Singapore
Chicago, IL	Brussels, Belgium	Melbourne, Australia	Stockholm, Sweden
Dallas, TX	Budapest, Hungary	Milan, Italy	Stuttgart, Germany
Los Angeles, CA	Buenos Aires, Argentina	Monterrey, Mexico	Sydney, Australia
New York, NY	Frankfurt, Germany	Moscow, Russia	Tokyo, Japan
San Francisco, CA	Hamburg, Germany	Mumbai, India	Toronto, Canada
Washington DC	Helsinki, Finland	Munich, Germany	Vienna, Austria
	Hong Kong	Oslo, Norway	Warsaw, Poland
	Jakarta, Indonesia	Paris, France	Zurich, Switzerland
	Kuala Lumpur, Malaysia	Sao Paulo, Brazil	
	Lisbon, Portugal	Seoul, South Korea	

What Don't They Like?

One area the firm could improve upon is its ability to "integrate new employees." Another mentioned the lack of overall supervision, while another said a job at BCG "requires a spirit of individualism and entrepreneurialism," and people who want to be told what to do all the time "need not apply."

Firm Evalutions

MBA Perceptions of BCG (*1-5 scale; 1=poor, 5=outstanding*)

	Prestige/ Reputation	Compensation	Long-Term Career Opportunities	Quality of Life
1999 Rating	★★★★★	★★★★★	★★★★★	★★★★★

Source: Kennedy Information Research Group's 1999 MBA Recruiting Study

Comments from MBA Students About BCG

Culture:	*Likes:*	*Dislikes:*
"Intellectual"	"Intelligent people, interesting work"	"Lack of quantitative rigor in analysis"
"Introverted"		
"Elite"	"Intellectual challenge"	"Little feedback"
"Friendly, open, laid back"	"Client base"	"Consultants do two cases simultaneously"
"Analytical"	"Creativity emphasized"	

Leadership Notes

Who knows? Twenty-three years after you graduate from B-school to join BCG, you might be the CEO. At least that's what happened to Carl Stern, who was at the top of his class at Stanford GSB in 1974 and was elected CEO and president in April 1997. He officially assumed the post January 1, 1998. He succeeded John Clarkeson, who had been CEO since 1985 and announced he wouldn't seek a fifth term when elected in 1994 (BCG officers elect a new chief executive every three years). Clarkeson remains on board as chairman.

Conclusion

Question: If there were any advice you would give to a new hire or summer associate about to enter BCG, what would it be?

"Ride out the difficult start, because there is a lot of fun, rewards, and learning to be had."

— male former consultant

"I would say speak up and let your ideas be known. Take an active role in choosing what you want to work on, and be grabby in terms of responsibility."

— 30-year-old female manager

CAMBRIDGE TECHNOLOGY PARTNERS

at a glance

Year Founded:	1991
Headquarters:	Cambridge, MA
1998 Consulting Revenues:	$612 million
Key Players:	Jack Messman, President, CEO
Number of Consultants:	4,500
Web Page:	www.ctp.com
Recruiting Contact:	Melissa Gibbons, Corporate Recruiter
Address:	304 Vassar Street Cambridge, MA 02139
Phone, Fax:	Ph: 617-374-8365, Fx: 617-374-8300

About the Firm

Cambridge Technology Partners (CTP) is a global systems integration and management consulting firm, the latter services provided through its Cambridge Management Consulting practice, which is under the CTP umbrella. (In 1997, CTP merged with UK-based Peter Chadwick Incorporated, creating the division of Cambridge Management Consulting.)

The firm is publicly traded (NASDAQ:CATP), and was riding high through the summer of 1998, trading in the high fifties. But the price plummeted below 20 during the fall of 1998, and its recovery has been glacial. At one point, CTP denied rumors of an exodus of staff due to worthless stock options. All of this suggests that working for a publicly owned consulting firm has an extra layer of excitement.

We have to hand it to a firm that says why it's different on its Web site. Sure, lots of firms do this, but mostly with meaningless corporate jargon. CTP lists its differences in succinct bullet points:

- An innovation focus
- A speed focus
- A project-based fee approach

The last point is perhaps the most relevant, since most firms can't or won't perform fixed-fee assignments, instead keeping the "meter running" with hourly, daily, or monthly billing.

CTP currently has 53 offices and 4,500 employees worldwide. The firm did $612 million in revenues in 1998, up an impressive 40% over the prior year, making CTP one of the fastest growing on *Consultants News*' 1999 largest firm ranking.

Services

CTP provides systems integration services, which include the following:

- Enterprise Resource Solutions (ERS)
- Interactive Solutions
- Customer Management Solutions
- Custom Software Solutions
- Cambridge Network Services
- IT Strategy and Planning
- Cambridge Educational Services
- Cambridge Application Maintenance and Support

The firm also maintains the Cambridge Information Network — an on-line research, advisory, and consulting services unit — and The Cambridge Management Lab, which provides executive education.

Management consulting is provided by Cambridge Management Consulting (CMC), delivering services such as:

- Asset Management
- Asset Optimization
- Customer Loyalty
- Knowledge Management
- Organizational Effectiveness
- Product and Process Leadership
- Value Chain Management
- Technology ROI
- Web Enabled Business Solutions

Both units (CTP and CMC) serve the following vertical industries:

- Automotive
- Chemicals
- Consumer Goods
- Electronics
- Engineering
- Financial Services
- High Tech
- Oil and Gas
- Transportation
- Utilities

Career Paths

The rungs of the corporate ladder at CTP are associate developer, developer, senior developer, technical team leader, project manager, and program manager. CMC has the following career steps: business analyst, senior business analyst, project manager, and client partner. The firm generally doesn't hire people "right out of school," unless the individual has prior consulting experience. One CMC consultant says the "minimum experience [of a candidate] is two years." CTP says the average consultant age is 31, while the average consultant age at CMC is 33. The firm claims to not have "typical" paths, and the duration of time between titles "varies" and depends on the skills and talent of the individual.

Training

The firm has a New Employee Orientation (NEO) program for new hires at all levels. The week-long program involves "learning the Cambridge culture," teaming exercises, and basically "learning how Cambridge does consulting." The following week, consultants go to a business-unit specific "boot camp" to learn CMC- or CTP-specific methodologies for the kind of work they will be doing. Ideally, the firm wants new hires to attend boot camp "right off the bat," but "the business reality is sometimes we don't have that luxury." A consultant may be put on a project right away and be unable to attend boot camp until after they have been at the firm for six months or longer. But the preference is to "get these people scheduled [for boot camp] as soon as they come in the door."

Summer Program

Cambridge Management Consulting does not have a summer program, but the firm offers internships to first year MBAs. It is a small, informal program. CMC claims it usually hires 80% of its interns when their educational commitment is completed.

Recruiting

CTP recruits at 75 colleges in the US and over 100 worldwide. A useful list of the schools, visit dates, and preferred degrees can be found on the firm's Web site under the "College Relations Program" heading. There is a "very generous" tuition reimbursement plan at CTP.

Compensation

In addition to the starting base salaries (see table), the firm offers a benefits program that it claims is "among the most competitive in the industry." Benefits include health, dental, life insurance, short-long-term disability insurance, year-end bonus, 401(k) plan, and those volatile stock options. Starting salaries vary according to the level of consulting experience you bring to the firm.

Salary Data

	Minimum Starting Base Salaries (1999)	Bonus (1999)
BA/BS	$40,000	N/A
MBA	$85,000	$5,000

Source: Cambridge Technology Partners and Kennedy Information/Consultants News

Office Life

The firm is "very much of a workaholic organization, but not in a bad way." Titles pertain more to your role on a client project and have little place in the office. People "feel like peers" instead of co-workers, and "everyone feels pretty much on par with everybody else" in terms of discourse. The atmosphere is not very competitive, and the consultants "tend to take their work seriously and take it very personally, so there is a very good work ethic here."

The average workweek is "about sixty" hours with an "unusual workweek of seventy-five to eighty." As it is with most firms, single people "do a little more work" than consultants with families. Travel "depends on where your clients are," but doesn't seem to get too grueling. You have "flexibility of schedule," which includes leaving to do personal things, and when possible, work time can be flexible.

Geographic Locations

US Locations

Allston, MA
Atlanta, GA
Bridgewater, NJ
Cambridge, MA
Chicago, IL
Columbus, OH
Dallas, TX
Detroit, MI
Miami, FL
Minneapolis, MN
New York, NY
Philadelphia, PA
Phoenix, AZ
Pittsburgh, PA
San Francisco, CA
San Mateo, CA
San Ramon, CA
Seattle, WA
Washington, DC

Non-US Office Locations

Amsterdam, The Netherlands
Bangalore, India
Brussels, Belgium
Frankfurt, Germany
Geneva, Switzerland
Linkoping, Sweden
Melbourne, Australia
Mexico City, Mexico
Munich, Germany
San Juan, Puerto Rico
Sao Paulo, Brazil
Stockholm, Sweden
Utrecht, The Netherlands
Vienna, Austria

What Don't They Like?

CTP is another young, fast-growth firm that has a relatively weak internal infrastructure, so "people who depend on structure" and are unable to handle ambiguity and a great deal of independence may be happier elsewhere. But if you are "flexible on what you do and where and when you do it" and don't necessarily need "clearly defined authority," CTP might have what you're looking for. Best thing about working for the firm? One word: "freedom."

Firm Evaluations

MBA Perceptions of CTP (*1-5 scale; 1=poor, 5=outstanding*)

	Prestige/Reputation	Compensation	Long-Term Career Opportunities	Quality of Life
1999 Rating	**	***	**	***

Source: Kennedy Information Research Group's 1999 MBA Recruiting Study

Comments from MBA Students About Cambridge Technology Partners

Culture:	*Likes:*	*Dislikes:*
"Workaholic"	"Lack of hierarchy"	"Weak internal systems"
"Young"	"Work flexibility"	"Lack of guidance"
"Fast"	"Autonomy, freedom"	"Hours"
"Results-oriented"		

Leadership Notes

James K. Sims had been leading Cambridge Technology Partners since it was formed in 1991. Before he joined CTP, he was the founder of Concurrent Computer Corporation, and led the firm's positioning away from standards-based systems to real-time computing applications. As CEO, James Sims predicted CTP would be a $2 billion company by 2002. Sims, however, met his demise as CEO after the firm badly missed an earnings estimate in early 1999 and he was roundly criticized for dumping his own CTP stock. Sims was replaced midyear by Jack Messman, who was formerly the president and CEO of Union Pacific Resources Group Inc. His lack of consulting experience has not gone unnoticed, but he may very well be the one to bring CTP successfully into the future.

Conclusion

Question: If there were any advice you could give to a new hire or summer associate going into CTP, what would it be?

"In the beginning, you've got the most time you'll probably ever have to learn about the company and learn where things are. Before you get put on assignments, go looking around in file cabinets and finding other resources, so when the time comes for you to need it, you'll know where to go."
— 42-year-old male consultant, Cambridge Management Consulting

COMPUTER SCIENCES CORPORATION (CSC)

at a glance

Year Founded:	1959
Headquarters:	El Segundo, CA
1998 Consulting Revenues:	$3.0 billion
Key Players:	Van Honeycut, President and CEO
	Kirk Arnold, CSC Consulting President
Number of Consultants:	20,000
Web Page:	www.csc.com
Recruiting Contact	
(no resumes):	Recruiting-manager@csc.com
Address:	2100 East Grand Ave.
	El Segundo, CA
Phone, Fax:	Ph: 310-615-0311, Fx: 310-322-9805

About the Firm

CSC was founded in 1959 and had total 1998 revenues of about $7.7 billion, of which $3.0 billion was generated by consulting services. The IT-oriented firm offers systems integration and other consulting services, and previously offered strategy consulting services through its CSC Index arm until mid-1998, when the Index name was dropped and the group was integrated into the rest of the firm. It likely wouldn't have happened — or at least been put off for a few years — if the Index brand name hadn't been indelibly associated with business process reengineering, an aging consulting craze. Ironic that Index "rode the reengineering wave and got caught in its undertow" as *Consultants News* observed at the time. The firm is active in R&D with its CSC Vanguard and Research and Advisory groups. CSC also holds a major annual conference, CSC Exchange, which draws about 1,000 execs a year.

Services

CSC provides IT, operations management, and strategy consulting services. About 40% of the firm's revenues are derived from outsourcing. CSC serves most industries and is especially strong in government (its roots), insurance, financial services, and manufacturing.

Career Paths

The firm is one that likes the title "associate." MBAs are known as "MBA associates" and undergraduates are just "associates." MBAs most often are on the strategic end of work, while undergraduates tend to have "a strong systems focus." After getting your feet wet, the firm wants you to "focus on a particular industry or a particular functional area."

Relatively "unstructured" training varies according to the background of the consultant and the line of business he or she is entering. One consultant who joined the firm was "put on a project my first day," but generally undergraduates tend to go through a "rigorous 10-week training program." Responsibility comes quickly for new MBA hires. Depending on the firm's needs and the background of a new hire, a new consultant could be shown where the bathroom is and orientation would be over.

Summer Program

CSC has an intern program for MBAs in their first year. For entry into the summer program, you must meet stringent qualifications, including minimum GPA requirements.

Recruiting

The firm recruits at over 100 graduate and undergraduate schools around the country. When CSC comes on campus, the presentation is a "typical one-hour Q&A session" that can "open your eyes as to how big CSC really is." (See chart on page 77 for schools where CSC recruits.)

Number of Employees Hired 1998–1999

	Actual (*academic yr. ending: 6/1999*)
BA/BS/MBA	1,000+

Source: CSC and Kennedy Information/Consultants News

Compensation

According to recent MBA hires, the range for starting compensation is "$72K to $80K, not including the signing bonus or the year-end bonus." The firm offers standard medical, vacation, and other benefits as part of its package. CSC mentions compensation on its Web page, indicating that it administers surveys to make sure comp packages for new hires are up to industry standards. As CSC says: "We've hired thousands of employees over the last five years. We must be doing something right to attract these people! Come find out for yourself!"

Office Life

CSC's culture is why some consultants choose the firm. "I had offers that paid significantly more," but after feeling "right at home" in the Cleveland office, one consultant accepted an offer there. Travel and hours are always "defined by the

Schools From Which CSC Actively Recruits

Arizona State U.
Austin College
Baylor University
Bentley College
Boston College
Boston University
Bowie State University
Bradley University
Brown University
Bryant College
California State Polytechnic State U.
California State University (Long Beach, Dominguez Hills, Fullerton)
Carleton College
Carnegie Mellon University
Central Connecticut University
Central Michigan University
Central Missouri State University
Christopher Newport University
College of St. Olaf
Colorado State U.
Columbia University
Cornell
De Vry Institute of Technology
DePaul University
Drexel University
Eastern Connecticut State University
Eastern Illinois University
Eastern Michigan University
Elmhurst College
Emporia State University
Florida International University
Florida State University
George Mason University
Gustavus Adolphus College
Harvard University
Illinois Institute of Technology
Illinois State University
Indiana University of Pennsylvania
Iowa State University
Johns Hopkins University
Kansas State
Lawrence Technological University
Lehigh University
Lincoln University
Louisiana State University
Louisiana Tech
Loyola University
Miami University
Michigan State University
Morgan State University
New England College
New York University
Northern Illinois University
Northwestern
Oakland University
Ohio State University
Ohio University
Oklahoma State University
Old Dominion University
Penn State University
Princeton University
Providence College
Quinnipiac College
Rensselaer Polytechnic Institute
Rice University
Rowan College
Rutgers University
Sam Houston State University
San Diego State University
Southern Connecticut State
Southwest Texas State University
Stephen F. Austin
Stockton State College
SUNY (Albany, Utica)
Tarleton State University
Texas A&M
Texas Christian University
Texas Tech University
Three Rivers Technical College
Trenton State College
Tulane University
University of Alabama
University of Arizona
University of Arkansas
University of California (San Diego, Santa Cruz, Berkeley)
University of Central Florida
University of Colorado
University of Connecticut
University of Dallas
University of Dayton
University of Florida
University of Houston
University of Illinois (Commerce, Engineering)
University of Iowa
University of Kansas
University of Maine
University of Maryland at College Park
University of Maryland, Baltimore County
University of Massachusetts
University of Michigan
University of Minnesota Institute of Technology
University of Missouri (Columbia, Rolla,
Washington U. School of Engineering)
University of North Texas
University of Oklahoma
University of Pittsburgh
University of Rhode Island
University of South Florida
University of Southern Louisiana
University of St. Thomas
University of Texas (Austin, San Antonio, Arlington, El Paso)
University of Vermont
University of Virginia
University of West Florida
University of Wisconsin (Madison, Eau Claire)
University of Wyoming
Vanderbilt University
Virginia Polytechnic Institute
Walsh College
Wayne State University
Western New England University
Yale University

Source: CSC and Kennedy Information/Consultants News

customer" and the firm does "whatever we need to do to please the client." Twelve-hour days are common, but weekends are "sacred" for most of the consultants. Camaraderie is found in project teams as well as in the office; one memorable Friday afternoon for one consultant was when some consultants went out and got "certain beverages" and then returned and the whole office "hung around drinking" and talking about their projects.

However, "only certain kinds" of people would like the firm, especially people who "prefer structure." Another consultant mentioned that potential new hires are brought on board only if they pass the "airplane test": If you can imagine yourself sitting on a plane with this person for hours on end and not being horrified, the person is in. (The infamous airplane test is referred to by many firms.)

Geographic Locations

CSC has 844 offices worldwide. Any of the regional offices would be willing to give you information on the closest offices to you.

CSC Office	City	Phone
Corporate Office	El Segundo, CA	310-615-0311
Consulting Group	Cambridge, MA	617-661-0900
CSC Credit Services	Houston, TX	281-878-1900
Financial Services Group	Austin, TX	888-268-2677
Systems Group	Falls Church, VA	703-876-1000
Technology Management Group	Falls Church, VA	800-775-1272
European Group	Hampshire, UK	44-1252-363-000
CSC Australia	St. Leonards, Australia	61-2-99011111

Firm Evaluations

MBA Perceptions of CSC (*1-5 scale; 1=poor, 5=outstanding*)

	Prestige/ Reputation	Compensation	Long-Term Career Opportunities	Quality of Life
1999 Rating	**	**	*	**

Source: Kennedy Information Research Group's 1999 MBA Recruiting Study

Leadership Notes

It's fascinating and frightening to think that a little over two years after James Champy left Index to join Perot, the Index brand name vanished into thin air. Jim Saviano was chairman and CEO of the Consulting & Systems Integration division of CSC before becoming the president of the consulting group. In the summer of 1999, he semi-retired from the post to bolster the firm's e-commerce practice (full time) and Kirk Arnold replaced him as president. She was formerly a vice president of strategic services for CSC's consulting group. Van Honeycutt — the chairman, CEO, and president of CSC — joined the firm in 1975 as regional marketing manager for the firm's timesharing and value-added network.

Conclusion

Question: If there were any advice you would give to a new hire or summer associate going into CSC, what would it be?

"Build your reputation as quickly as you can. Your rep will carry you through CSC. Once you build that, it opens doors around the company."
— 28-year-old male consultant

DELOITTE CONSULTING

at a glance

Year Founded:	1947
Headquarters:	New York, NY
1998 Consulting Revenues:	$3.2 billion
Key Players:	Doug McCracken, Chairman for US & National Managing Director
Number of Consultants:	19,560
Web Page:	www.deloitte.com
Recruiting Contacts:	John Worth, MBA Contact Jennifer Lemalgre, Systems Analysts (Undergrad) Tracey Dumas, Business Analysts (Undergrad)
Address:	150 Fayette St. Mall, Suite 1800 Raleigh, NC 27602
Phone, Fax:	Ph: 919-546-8046, Fx: 919-346-8096

About the Firm

Deloitte Consulting is the consulting unit of Deloitte Touche Tohmatsu, which has 63,450 employees in 126 countries. Deloitte & Touche (the "Tohmatsu" name is seldom used in the US) was born in 1989 when Deloitte, Haskins & Sells merged with Touche Ross. The firm has one of the best reputations of the Big Five in terms of lifestyle: *Fortune* magazine in 1998 ranked the firm number 14 in its annual ranking of the 100 Best Companies to Work For In America. Deloitte also ranked best of the Big Five in terms of lifestyle in Kennedy Information's 1998 MBA recruiting study, coming in 4th overall in 1998 and proving this was no fluke by jumping to 2nd in 1999.

The firm is moving faster than ever before in terms of branding, continuing with an aggressive "them" and "us" marketing campaign initially launched in 1997. Deloitte has ambitious plans of wanting to establish itself as "the third major global consulting brand," alongside McKinsey and Andersen Consulting. Also, the firm has been undistracted by external events, compared to the rest of the Big Five. In the last few years, E&Y and KPMG announced merger plans that later collapsed, Price Waterhouse and Coopers & Lybrand merged, and Andersen Consulting and Arthur Andersen are mired in divorce proceedings. Deloitte has played off this state of disarray in ads such as: "Which Big Six firm will spend next year focusing on your problems, not theirs?"

Services

Deloitte serves most industries, including manufacturing, consumer and business telecommunications and media, financial services, healthcare, utilities and energy, and the public sector. It has a strong presence in the enterprise resource planning software (e.g., SAP, Baan) implementation business, following its 1995 acquisition of ICS. Deloitte has developed new methodologies in SAP implementation, including FastTrack, IndustryPrint, and ValuePrint. It is now focusing on "second wave" work — how clients with SAP installations can get big business results from it. Its strategy arm (Braxton) recently folded into the rest of the firm, in part to help promote the Deloitte brand name.

Career Paths

MBAs start as senior consultants, and in one to three years become managers. An additional two to four years takes them to the senior manager level, and it is approximately three more years before becoming partner. Developing a career path is up to the individual, because according to recruits, "you could be a partner in five years or ten years," but not many people can "compress the [time to partner] to six years." Industry hires enter the firm as high as the partner level.

Undergrads come in as business analysts or systems analysts, then move up to associate consultants, and then senior consultants. It is common to return to business school after a period of 2-5 years at the firm.

Initially on assignments, you're exposed to different industries. The firm expects its consultants to be generalists for the first two years and specialize afterward, like choosing a major at the end of your sophomore year at college.

Training

The firm has "standardized national and local training," and new MBA senior consultants can expect a two-week-long training session in the firm's Florida facility. The first week addresses general consulting processes and methodologies, with "great things on presentations and listening skills," while the second week has more of a "strategy" focus. D&T does a "good job pulling it together" at the "very comprehensive and relevant" session and is constantly reviewing the training and its effectiveness.

Summer Program

MBAs entering the 10- to 12-week summer program act as senior consultants and serve clients through research, analysis, and presentations. There is a lot of "access to partners," and the summer associates admired Deloitte's "roll-up-their-sleeves approach." The basic purpose of the program is to "get a feel for the firm" and find out the Deloitte's positioning through "actual, real work." A summer intern who worked on two projects thought the firm did "a very good job creating an interesting working environment."

Recruiting

Deloitte recruits at 60 undergraduate universities in the US and looks for majors such as business, engineering, math, science, IT, and liberal arts. Its approach in recruiting is appreciated — according to sources, the firm has less of an "attitude" than some of the other firms. One student commented on how the "elite" firms have a "we're great and everybody else sucks" approach while "Deloitte has a very down-to-earth attitude."

Number of Employees Hired 1999–2000

	Actual (*academic yr. ending: 6/1999*)	Expected (*academic yr. ending: 6/2000*)	Summer Associates (*hired–1999*)
BA/BS	574	411	60
MBA	164	160	91
Industry Experts	1142	678	N/A

Source: Deloitte Consulting and Kennedy Information/Consultants News

On-Campus Recruiting (Graduate Level)

Schools from which the firm actively recruits	1998 Recruits
University of Chicago	15
Carnegie Mellon University	9
Columbia University	14
Darden	12
Fuqua	11
Harvard Business School	16
Kellogg	18
Kenan-Flagler	11
University of Michigan	22
University of Texas	15
UCLA	17
Wharton	24

Source: Deloitte Consulting and Kennedy Information/Consultants News

Compensation

According to one consultant, compensation at Deloitte is "competitive or exceeds competition in the early years," but after the third year, the pay isn't as high as some of the firm's competitors. The firm has experienced problems with turnover after year three, but is working on this. Either way, the firm wouldn't be for "someone who wants to be a millionaire in five years," although Deloitte partners are highly paid as are partners at most of the largest firms. The benefits package includes life and health insurance, 401(k) pension, family leave, dependent care, and flexible work arrangements.

Office Life

Around the office there is a real "down-to-earth sense and an intellectual curiosity." The people at the firm are "bright and don't pretend that they are something that they're not." The expression "great people" is a "common thing said about Deloitte staff." There is "a lot of camaraderie in the project teams and in the office." Some people inside and outside of project teams "get together every Thursday night" for dinner and hanging out. There are many events and receptions and the employees "do a lot of things as a group," but aren't obligated to participate; there is "no need for face time here."

The typical workweek, although there are "peaks and valleys," is "probably 50 to 60 hours a week," and there are many consultants who take advantage of flex time. Many people who "have small children will work three-quarters time or half time," an arrangement that "works very well." People at the firm "care about the work-life balance." Deloitte isn't for a "real hard charger who doesn't have a life." Another consultant believes "you're not going to kill yourself in consulting if you stay here." You might work an occassional weekend, but "it's something you need to take control of yourself."

Geographic Locations

US Locations	Non-US Locations	
Atlanta, GA	Adelaide, Australia	Osaka, Japan
Austin, TX	Amsterdam, The Netherlands	Oslo, Norway
Boston, MA	Aukland, New Zealand	Ottawa, Canada
Chicago, IL	Bangkok, Thailand	Perth, Australia
Cincinnati, OH	Bath, UK	Pretoria, South Africa
Cleveland, OH	Brisbane, Australia	Sao Paulo, Brazil
Dallas, TX	Buenos Aires, Argentina	Singapore
Detroit, MI	Calgary, Canada	Stockholm, Sweden
East Brunswick, NJ	Canberra, Australia	Strassen, Luxembourg
Houston, TX	Cedex, France	Sydney, Australia
Kansas City, MO	Conventry, UK	Tokyo, Japan
Los Angeles, CA	Copenhagen, Denmark	Toronto, Canada
Marietta, GA	Diegem, Belgium	Vancouver, Canada
Minneapolis, MN	Dusseldorf, Germany	Vienna, Austria
New York, NY	Helsinki, Finland	Wellington, New Zealand
Parsippany, NJ	Hong Kong	Zurich, Switzerland
Philadelphia, PA	Johannesburg, South Africa	
Pittsburgh, PA	Lisbon, Portugal	
Sacramento, CA	London, UK	
San Francisco, CA	Madrid, Spain	
Santa Ana, CA	Melbourne, Australia	
Seattle, WA	Mexico City, Mexico	
Stamford, CT	Milano, Italy	
Washington, DC	Monterrey, Mexico	
West Palm Beach, FL	Montreal, Canada	

What Don't They Like?

There are some "growing pains" associated with the absorption of strategy practice Braxton into Deloitte. Another mentioned that recognition in the marketplace could be "improved upon" — this is clearly being addressed by the somewhat controversial "Them and Us" ads. "It is a dynamite firm with incredible potential," and now that it started the ad campaign, it "can't let up on it." One consultant didn't like the fact that as a new consultant, you "cannot specialize along industry lines or service lines," but this is very much a matter of personal preference.

Firm Evaluation

MBA Perceptions of Deloitte Consulting (*1-5 scale; 1=poor, 5=outstanding*)

	Prestige/Reputation	Compensation	Long-Term Career Opportunities	Quality of Life
1999 Rating	*****	*****	*****	*****

Source: Kennedy Information Research Group's 1999 MBA Recruiting Study

Comments from MBA Students About Deloitte Consulting

Culture:	Likes:	Dislikes:
"Fun, challenging, surprising"	"Respect and recognition from management and partnership"	"Admin/support staff"
"Think differently"		"Management communication regarding compensation and strategy is limited"
"Good work life balance, family- oriented"	"More strategic work than expected"	
"Friendly, supportive, down to earth, warm"	"Team-oriented environment"	"Politics"
"Collegial and team-oriented"	"Opportunity for advancement"	"Not enough advisory work"
"Competitive and hard working"	"Bright people, friendly"	"Growing too fast"
		"Inconsistency across offices"

Leadership Notes

Pat Loconto is the CEO of Deloitte Consulting Worldwide, and it took two people to replace Mike Cook, who was chairman and CEO of Deloitte U.S.A. for fifteen years. Deloitte has the important distinction of being the first (mark our words: other firms will do the same, which is why we use the word "first" instead of "only") Big Five firm to appoint the job of chairman to a partner on the consulting side. Doug McCracken, 50, had been the leader of the Americas practice for Deloitte Consulting prior to his appointment of chairman, which happened in early 1999. James D. Copeland — from the audit/tax side — is succeeding Cook in the CEO slot.

Conclusion

Question: If there were any advice that you would give to a new hire or a summer associate going to work at Deloitte Consulting, what would it be?

"Just get to know people, start to develop your network. So much of staffing is based on that."

— 30-year-old male senior consultant

"Have fun, and use the people around you to learn as much as you can. If you work hard and are part of the team, you'll be successful."

— 33-year-old female senior consultant

DIAMOND TECHNOLOGY PARTNERS

at a glance

Year Founded:	1994
Headquarters:	Chicago, IL
1998 Revenues:	$584 million
Key Players:	Mel Bergstein, Chairman & CEO
Number of Consultants:	305
Web Page:	www.diamtech.com
Recruiting Contact:	Jill Marie Rupple
Address:	875 N. Michigan Avenue Chicago, IL 60611
Phone, Fax, e-mail:	Ph: 312-255-5000, Fx:312-255-6000

Partner & Professional Breakdown

# Partners	59
# Women Partners	5
# Minority Partners	8
# Professionals	305
# Women Professionals (exc. Partners)	62
# Minority Professionals (exc. Partners)	121

Source: Diamond Technology Partners and Kennedy Information/Consultants News

About the Firm

Diamond Technology Partners (DTP) was founded in 1994 by Melvyn Berstein and Christopher Moffitt, both from Technology Solutions Corp. Its value proposition has always been simple: using information technology as the driving force in devising and implementing business strategies. In some way, most IT firms have the same approach, but DTP was arguably the first to put it on paper.

DTP went public less than three years after it was founded (NASDAQ: DTPI), despite the fact that at the time its revenues were about half of its market capitalization and the firm had no profits. Regardless, the firm packaged itself well, went public at $5 per share, and is shining like a diamond in the public eye.

DTP has won praise from *Consultants News* for employing winning marketing and branding strategies. During 1998, the firm launched Diamond Exchange learning forum, the quarterly magazine *Context*, and the annual Digital Strategy Survey.

Services

DTP has brought areas of expertise such as e-commerce and Internet strategies to the center stage in its self-descriptions. Offerings include Digital Strategy, Program Management, Change Management, and Profit Improvement. The firm consults to most industries, including financial services, healthcare, manufacturing, utilities, and telecommunications.

Career Paths

The steps leading to partner are analyst, associate, principal, senior principal, and finally partner. DTP claims a new associate has the opportunity to become partner within six years. As at most firms, MBAs come in at the associate level, with undergrads coming in as analysts.

Training

DTP provides new hires with a number of programs to get their tools sharpened for the consulting thicket. Its "assimilation" program includes teaching skills such as industry research, business writing, and presentation development. On-the-job training is continuous, and after each consulting engagement, formal evaluations of consultants' skills are given by their superiors. If "opportunities for career development" arise from the evaluation, the superior will recommend appropriate training for the consultant.

Summer Program

During an eleven-week internship, summer associates work on one client project and are responsible for "identifying key issues, performing detailed analyses and formulating recommendations." One summer associate said she was "in contact with clients constantly" and thought the experience at the firm was completely worthwhile. (She plans to return to the firm as a full time consultant when she completes business school.)

Another summer associate said there was one day of training at the start of the summer, and you begin a client engagement the next day. Midsummer, she experienced a week of training on "how DTP is different" at its Chicago office, and thought it was good to "meet partners and get a real feel for the firm."

Summer Associate Data

Percentage of 1998 BA/BS summer associates were offered full time positions:	N/A
Percentage of offers made that were accepted:	N/A
Percentage of 1998 MBA summer associates were offered full time positions:	98%
Percentage of offers made that were accepted:	85%

Source: Diamond Technology Partners and Kennedy Information/Consultants News

Recruiting

Like many IT firms, in its recruiting process DTP is putting heavy emphasis on Internet and especially e-commerce interests, and hired almost as many industry experts in 1998 as it did MBAs. The on-campus recruiting style seemed to fare well; students said the recruiting director and others "provided substantial feedback" that "none of the other consulting firms, especially the big ones" provided.

Number of Employees Hired 1998-1999

	Actual (*academic yr. ending: 6/1999*)	**Expected** (*academic yr. ending: 6/2000*)	**Summer Associates** (*hired–1999*)
BA/BS	19	45	N/A
MBA	65	65	30
MA/PhD/other students	N/A	15	N/A
Industry Experts	75	100	N/A

Source: Diamond Technology Partners and Kennedy Information/Consultants News

Compensation

Compensation, especially when options are considered, is "very competitive," but as with some equity compensation plans, the longer you're there, "the better off you'll be." Another source echoed similar sentiments, saying "the salary probably isn't the highest" but with the equity, it is likely a "big advantage." Another benefit worth mentioning is the comprehensive health plan, with one consultant saying she hasn't "spent a penny on health care in the three years since I've worked at Diamond."

Office Life

An interesting attribute of DTP — which plays into the ever present "lifestyle" issue — is the fact that it claims its consultants can live anywhere they want to, "as long as it's near an airport." One consultant chimed in: "DTP is headquartered in Chicago, which is beautiful, with a view of Lake Michigan and downtown Chicago." Another consultant thinks "less than 30% of the DTP staff lives in Chicago." The rationale of having no other offices and having this flexible living option policy is if a consultant is "away from home all the time, there is no point in having an office."

Though there are no offices to return to, DTP consultants pride themselves on having a strong culture, which is described by one consultant as "open" and that consultants get together "several times a year for all-hands meeting to share information." The meetings are centered around quarterly earnings announcements, and are "open discussions about the firm's direction." With every consultant having equity, there is a "feeling of ownership" among the staff. This ownership culture appears to be very strong. One consultant said "there have been a couple of attempts to do mass raids on our troops which have proven unsuccessful. People like it here."

The average work week for most is fifty-hours, with sixty hours per week expected "when something is due." Travel is twice a week — once to go to the client site, once to come back—usually on Mondays and Fridays. A consultant noted that one thing DTP does extremely well is assembling small consulting teams because the firm "prefers the SWAT team approach as opposed to the schoolbus approach" because there aren't "a bazillion Diamond people on the ground."

What Don't They Like?

One consultant was concerned DTP would lose the culture as it grows, because people "like the small firm feel." Another consultant had similar sentiments, saying the firm needed to maintain "a strong focus on who we are" but quickly added that DTP "has a good grip on it, but it is a concern."

Firm Evaluations

MBA Rating (*1-5 scale; 1=poor, 5=outstanding*)

	Prestige/ Reputation	Compensation	Long-Term Career Opportunities	Quality of Life
1999 Rating	****	****	*****	****

Source: Kennedy Information Research Group's 1998 MBA Recruiting Study

Leadership Notes

Mel Bergstein, who founded DTP, doesn't appear to be close to retiring. However, he has been in the professional services game for a while — 21 years with Arthur Andersen (and Andersen Consulting), three years at CSC, and another three at TSC. Bergstein has a B.S. in Economics from The Wharton School and is also a certified public accountant.

Conclusion

Question: If there was any advice you'd give to a new consultant or a summer associate going into Diamond Technology Partners, what would it be?

"Don't be afraid to make mistakes. Be honest when saying what you do and don't know. I think people bring baggage from other firms, so my advice is: leave your baggage at the door, this is a different place."

— 33 year old female consultant

"Come with an open mind. Don't let the fact that it's a small firm with less brand recognition in the marketplace be a deterrent — there's tremendous growth potential here."

— 28 year old female consultant

"The kind of work we get is interesting, but we're also laying the groundwork to do exciting work that we all want to do in the future. See the big picture and be patient — recognize this is a firm in growth mode."

— 33 year old male consultant

ERNST & YOUNG

at a glance

Year Formed:	1989
Headquarters:	New York, NY
1998 Consulting Revenues:	$3.8 billion
Key Players:	Phil Laskawy, Chief Executive Officer
	Terry Ozan, CEO, Ernst & Young Consulting Worldwide
Number of Consultants:	16,450
Web Page:	www.ey.com
Recruiting Contacts by Region	
Atlanta Area: Atlanta, Charlotte & Tampa	Ph: 404-874-8300, Fx: 404-817-4244
	E-mail: atlantamcrecruiting@ey.com
Chicago Area: Chicago, Minneapolis & Milwaukee	Ph: 312-879-2000, Fx: 312-879-3892
	E-mail: mcchic@ey.com
Cleveland Area: Cleveland, Detroit, Pittsburgh, Cincinnati, Indianapolis & Columbus	Ph: 216-861-5000, Fx: 216-737-1810
	E-mail: mcclev@ey.com
Dallas Area: Dallas, Ft. Worth & Irving	Ph: 214-665-5000, Fx: 214-665-5300
	E-mail: mcdfw@ey.com
Houston Area:	Ph: 713-750-1500, Fx: 713-750-8646
	E-mail: mchous@ey.com
Los Angeles Area:	Ph: 213-977-3200, Fx: 213-683-1269
New York/Boston Area:	Ph: 212-773-3000, Fx: 212-733-3000
Philadephia Area: Philadelphia, Fairfax, Washington D.C. & Baltimore	Ph: 215-448-5000, Fx; 215-448-2627
San Francisco Area: St. Louis, Kansas City & Denver	Ph: 314-259-1000, Fx: 314-259-1618
	E-mail: stload@ey.com

About the Firm

Number three in the Big Five, behind PwC and Andersen Worldwide (in terms of total revenues), Ernst & Young (E&Y) was formed in 1989 after the merger of Arthur Young & Co. and Ernst & Whinney – the last of the mergers in the 1980s that turned the Big Eight into the Big Six. Parent organization Ernst & Young International employs 72,000 people at 660 locations around the world. E&Y maintains a "Global Client Consulting" group, which allows multinational consulting clients to have one point of contact at the firm. Like the rest of the Big Five, the firm is now shying away from the A-word — accounting — in its self-descriptions, preferring instead "professional services firm." Since consulting revenues grew at 35% for 1998 while the audit/tax division grew at a far slower rate, it's a justified change of description.

The firm has a new global branding ad campaign, which is often seen in the pages of *The Wall Street Journal*. Like the other members of the Big Five, E&Y recognizes the need both to boost awareness of its name as a consulting operation, and to present a consistent image throughout the world. This requires the firm to overcome what historically were independent national practices operating fairly independently.

E&Y was also named one of the 100 best companies to work for by *Working Mother* magazine. This is an important distinction for consulting firms with notoriously tough lifestyles. E&Y is justifiably proud of this recognition.

There has been little bad press about the firm, aside from what *Consultants News* called "Post-Merger Panic." In what seemed like a knee-jerk reaction, the firm announced a merger with KPMG Peat Marwick within weeks of the Price Waterhouse/Coopers & Lybrand announcement. After a few months tooting their horns about how "one plus one is more than two" the firms called off the wedding due to problems with "worldwide regulators."

Services

E&Y is a global firm with broad consulting capabilities, with particular strength in information technology and operations management. It serves most industries through nine practices. E&Y maintains several Centers for Business Knowledge (CBKs), a Center for Business Innovation (CBI), and a Center for Business Transformation (CBT). A few years ago, it launched "Internet consultant" *Ernie*, a concept which has since been duplicated by some competitors. Subscribers to *Ernie* can pose questions and tap into E&Y's network to get quick, expert answers. The firm also sponsors the annual "Entrepreneur of the Year" prize.

Career Paths

During their first year, new hires are assigned to a functional team according to the firm's needs and the individual's skills. Individual experience, competencies, and interests help determine the projects on which new hires will work and the responsibilities they will be assigned.

An individual who joins the firm with a bachelor's degree begins as a staff consultant. His/her career then progresses to the senior consultant, manager, senior manager, and finally principal or partner levels. Individuals with graduate degrees and/or relevant work experience typically enter the firm as senior consultants.

Training

For new hires entering the firm with a bachelor's degree, the foundation course is a 16-day "Consultant Entry Program." New hires with a graduate degree or relevant work experience attend the 10-day "Consulting for the Advanced Practitioner" program. Additional training follows each year thereafter.

Summer Program

E&Y's summer internship program lasts approximately 10 weeks. Most interns receive training and are assigned to client engagements where they learn on-site and contribute to the project. During the summer experience, interns also have the opportunity to participate in social and educational events with other interns. The interns "probably average 50 hours a week" and, on the whole, like the program. Objectives aren't over-defined and the firm "wants to see us assessed in the best way possible and learn as much as we can." Prior to the program, summer associates complete a form outlining what they want to accomplish during the internship.

Summer Associate Data

Percentage of 1998 BA/BS summer associates who were offered full-time positions: 85%

Source: Ernst & Young and Kennedy Information/Consultants News

Recruiting

E&Y's figures speak for themselves in terms of on-campus recruiting. As the third largest consulting firm, E&Y recruits at most MBA (and many undergrad) campuses around the world. Contact the regional recruiting manager nearest you to find out if and when the firm is coming to your school.

Number of Employees Hired 1998–1999

	Actual (academic yr. ending: 6/1999)
BA/BS	521
MBA	213
MA/PhD/Other Students	113

Source: Ernst & Young and Kennedy Information/Consultants News

Compensation

In addition to base salaries, which are on par with industry averages, E&Y offers Results-Based Performance and Rewards (RBPR), an incentive compensation plan designed to provide rewards where predetermined goals have been met. Additional compensation may also include tuition reimbursement and participation in the firm's 401(k) plan. The compensation overall is "competitive" and was "much more than I was expecting," according to one satisfied consultant. One summer associate thought it was "very good" and was paid hourly, receiving between $12 and $17 per hour. Signing bonuses for consultants are the norm, but one complaint was that "you aren't eligible for the 401(k) plan until after a year has passed."

Salary Data

	Average Starting Salary (1999)	Average Bonus
BA/BS	$48,645	$3,000
MBA	$76,399	$15,000

Source: E&Y and Kennedy Information/Consultants News

Office Life

At most offices, if you're a manager or below, you're in a cubicle. If you're a senior manager or above, you're in an office. The office in St. Louis, for example, is "pretty open with mostly cubicles" and "enough privacy to create your own little space and enough openness for good communication." The Dallas office, where there are about 200 consultants, is "not bad" in its layout, and "there are not a lot of people there because most consultants are at client sites."

The firm's culture is "very accepting — very easy to fit in." E&Y people are described as "very friendly," while the level of camaraderie "depends on the project." On occasion, "if it's someone's birthday, we'll get a cake for them, or we'll go to lunch." After hours, consultants often go out for drinks, "especially if someone's in from out of town." Many consultants "would recommend this firm to most anyone, but you have to be a team player, and this firm tries to foster that type of environment." Despite all of the titles, the firm has a structure that is "pretty flat," and it's "common knowledge that you have access to just about anything and anybody."

Geographic Locations

E&Y has presence in 132 countries, with 87 offices in the U.S. The regional recruiting contacts will provide information on the offices closest to you.

What Don't They Like?

HR was an issue: "The hiring process is very unorganized," says one, and HR systems are "pretty poor," with problems "getting through the paperwork."

There was sometimes seemingly unnecessary "stress levels that resulted from fire-drill handling of projects — everything last minute and critical." (Fire-drills are common at most firms. Get used to it.) Another consultant would have "preferred more direct client exposure in the early stages." Getting more people involved in social events would be welcomed, and getting on a desired project can be "hit or miss." (Again, get used to it.)

Firm Evaluations

MBA Perceptions of Ernst & Young (*1-5 scale; 1=poor, 5=outstanding*)

	Prestige/ Reputation	Compensation	Long-Term Career Opportunities	Quality of Life
1999 Rating	****	****	****	****

Source: Kennedy Information Research Group's 1999 MBA Recruiting Study

Comments from MBA Students About Ernst & Young

Culture:	*Likes:*	*Dislikes:*
"Motivated, dynamic"	"Willingness to share and opportunity to grow"	"Confusing business structure"
"Collaborative"		
"Professional, conservative"	"Social, appreciative people"	"Administration"
"Value-based, implementation"	"Assignments that keep you from moving on"	"Weak reputation in strategy work"
"Teamwork, friendly environment"	"Work with colleagues worldwide"	"Compensation"
		"Process-focused red tape"
"Entrepreneurial, young"	"Challenging, diverse work"	
	"Flexibility"	

Leadership Notes

Philip A. Laskawy, chairman and CEO of E&Y, was elected to a second term as chairman and CEO in July of 1997. His second term ends September 30, 2001. He is also a member of the Independence Standards Board, which was created by the American Institute of Certified Public Accountants (AICPA) and the Securities and Exchange Commission (SEC). The ISB is truly an important organization—some of the Big Five have raised serious conflict of interest issues by providing audit services for clients they provide consulting for or vice versa. The ISB is the entity working to resolve these issues.

Terry Ozan, the CEO of E&Y Consulting Worldwide, replaced Roger Nelson in September of 1999. Nelson was the vice chairman of management consulting, and the new title bestowed to Ozan could indicate reorg in E&Y's future.

Conclusion

Question: If there were any advice you would give to a new hire or a summer associate coming into Ernst & Young, what would it be?

"Number one: Make sure you network and participate in as many activities as you can. Number two is be flexible and try out the different things you want to try out. It may take several years, but find a niche."

— 24-year-old male full-time consultant

"Learn as much as you can. Period."

— male summer associate

"Make sure you like implementation. If you want to do strategy, you won't be happy. Take advantage of the network; the people are very friendly."

— 27-year-old female summer associate

GEMINI CONSULTING

at a glance

Year Founded:	1991
Headquarters:	Paris, France
1998 Consulting Revenues:	$400 million (KI estimate)
Key Players:	Serge Kampf, Chairman, Cap Gemini
	Tony Robinson, Gemini Consulting
Web Page:	www.gemcon.com
Recruiting Contact:	Karleen Mussman
Address:	Gemini Consulting
	25 Airport Road
	Morristown, NJ
Contact Information:	Ph: 973-285-9000
	E-mail: gemini.recruiting.US@gemcon.com

About the Firm

Gemini Consulting was formed in 1991, when Gemini acquired United Research, then later merged with the MAC Group to form Gemini Consulting (GC). GC's real identity was associated with "transformation" initiatives, a faddish idea GC developed and carried for years, but isn't associated much with anymore. The firm recently acquired the European-based firm Bossard Consultants, which enhances its positioning in that marketplace. The firm is a wholly-owned subsidiary of Cap Gemini Group, a $5 billion IT services firm based in Paris. GC has only two offices in the U.S., but is still considered a "global" firm, with 1,800 consultants.

Services

The firm's strengths lie in operations and strategy consulting services, while the parent company handles much of the IT side. The firm's services line includes strategy, capital effectiveness, e-commerce, euro services, growth, knowledge management, leadership development, and supply chain management.

Career Paths

Undergrads are hired into Gemini Consulting as consultants, and after two or three years they could become senior consultants. If the firm "feels like you don't need to go back to business school," there's no need to leave for your MBA. As an undergraduate consultant, the firm is a "great place to apply a lot of different skills." MBA graduates are hired at the senior consultant level and begin their careers, in the firm's words, "designing and managing phases, or 'streams,' of client engagements."

Training

Gemini Consulting has a "good, but not excellent" training program for consultants joining the firm; one consultant felt the training was a bit basic. Out of the gate, you have two weeks of training about skills and "tools and things" at the firm. At Gemini University, you can "choose whatever courses you want." There are usually two training off-sites a year. Consultants like the training "because it's flexible and well structured."

Summer Program

At Gemini Consulting, summer interns join for about three months between May and early September, acting as full-time team members. Interns begin their experience with a three day "Gemini summer skills workshop" that is an overview of the firm and its methodologies, computer training, and helpful hints. Each intern is assigned a mentor who, with a project manager, evaluates the internship. The Gemini summer intern program (consisting of consultants, Gemini leadership, and individuals from the recruiting team) schedules special events during the summer for interns to receive more training, network with other interns, and meet full-time consultants. Gemini usually reviews first-year resumes for application to the summer program in late December and early January. Interviews are conducted in January and February.

Recruiting

Gemini Consulting recruits at the schools shown in the following chart.

Schools from which the firm actively recruits

Europe	United States
Bocconni	University of Chicago
Cambridge	Cornell
Cranfield	Carnegie Mellon University
Erasmus	Fuqua School of Business (Duke)
ESADE	Georgetown
HEC	Goizueta Business School (Emory)
IESE	Harvard
IMD	Kellogg
INSEAD	University of Michigan
London Business School	MIT
Loueven	NYU (Stern School)
Nijenroden	UPENN-Wharton
Oxford	The ECCD Consortium (Includes Amherst,
Rotterdam	Bowdoin, Colgate, Hamilton, Middlebury,
Sweden School of Economics	St. Lawrence, Skidmore, Wesleyan, and Williams)
U NOVA	

Source: Gemini Consulting and Kennedy Information/Consultants News

Compensation

In 1998, new Gemini Consulting MBAs started at about $90,000 base salary. According to one consultant, the firm's compensation is "on par with Boston Consulting Group or Bain" and "in comparison to a Kearney or Andersen, [compensation] is 10 to 15% higher." An MBA consultant in the UK earning 63,000 pounds, with a bonus of about 10%, said her salary was "very good." The firm has bonuses, flexible benefits, or "cafeteria plans" which vary by country and usually include options for family health, retirement/pension, and personal benefits. Tuition reimbursement "may be offered at the consultant level to the very top candidates." Further up the career ladder, a managing director earns about $350,000 —something to look forward to.

Office Life

Gemini Consulting is "very obsessive about quality around the clients" but all of the offices are "relaxed" and you can "be yourself." You could visit five different offices in five different countries, but "they'd all be the same — except for the accents." There "aren't a lot of politics," one consultant says.

One consultant in the US said Gemini's model is 100% travel: Getting on a plane on Monday means you come home Friday afternoon, although depending on the deliverables, "you might be home Thursday." However, a consultant in the UK said the firm adheres to the "5-4-3" rule that many firms have: Five days working for the client, four nights of travel, and three nights away from home. Certainly, you can expect to do a healthy amount of travel. Depending upon where you are, "people make it work" and some consultants love the weekend adventures and the thrill of being a "22-year-old with a plane ticket," because you can spend "one weekend on the slopes, and another weekend in the sun." During hard weeks of traveling, it comes down to: "Do I enjoy the people I'm with?"

There are ups and downs with the work hours but the average Gemini consultant "wouldn't keep crazy hours for more than two weeks." The firm is "extremely flexible in its attitude toward people" and "your personal life can determine what projects you'll be on." The firm allows reduced work schedules and developed a flexible work program, called FlexForce, which is a sabbatical program that allows consultants to take a few months off to "refresh and rejuvenate" or work on a "compressed nine, ten, or eleven-month work schedule." The firm is also trying to make sure the reduced work schedule "isn't just a woman thing."

This firm would be "the right place" for someone who "wants to do strategy and implement it" and for anyone who wants "accountability and responsibility right out of the gate." The consultants at GC are "definitely not report writers" and the firm gives its consultants "just enough support to succeed in the workplace."

Geographic Locations:

US Locations	Non-US Locations	
Boston, MA	Barcelona, Spain	Milan, Italy
New York, NY	Berlin, Germany	Munich, Germany
	Brussels, Belgium	Oslo, Norway
	Bucharest, Hungary	Paris, France
	Cologne, Germany	Riga, Latvia
	Copenhagen, Denmark	St. Petersburg, Russia
	Frankfurt, Germany	Singapore
	Helsinki, Finland	Stockholm, Sweden
	Johannesburg, South Africa	Tokyo, Japan
	Lisbon, Portugal	Utrecht, Netherlands
	London, England	Vienna, Austria
	Lyon, France	Warsaw, Poland
	Madrid, Spain	Zurich, Switzerland

Firm Evaluations

MBA Perceptions of Gemini Consulting (*1-5 scale; 1=poor, 5=outstanding*)

	Prestige/ Reputation	Compensation	Long-Term Career Opportunities	Quality of Life
1999 Rating	****	****	****	**

Source: Kennedy Information Research Group's 1999 MBA Recruiting Study

Comments from MBA Students About Gemini Consulting

Culture:	Likes:	Dislikes:
"Technical orientation"	"Deep pockets"	"Little professional development"
"Balanced work life"	"Opportunities for advancement"	"Not a strong culture or training"
"Entrepreneurial, collegial, international"	"People, projects, career opportunities"	"Travel"
"Processy, but very capable"	"Sheer ability"	"Some decision-making processes"
		"Creates Identikits" (cookie cutter solutions)

Leadership Notes

Patrick J. Elder, the former CEO of Gemini Consulting, retired at age 52 to "spend more time with his family and pursue non-business interests." He was GC's CEO only from March 1997 to December 1998, but has a lot to show for it in terms of revenue growth. He is also responsible for the successful integration of Bossard Consultants and Gemini Consulting. Elder's successor, Tony Robinson, has been with Cap Gemini UK as head of the IT services and consulting practice. Robinson himself also led Cap Gemini UK through rapid revenue growth.

Conclusion

Question: If there were any advice you would give to a new hire or summer associate going into Gemini Consulting, what would it be?

"Talk to as many people in the firm as possible. Ask all the hard questions, don't take things at face value. Make sure you get all your questions answered."
— 30-year-old male senior consultant

"Use your mentor — because it is a big company — and find out which project role is right for you. Don't be scared to ask questions."
— 26-year-old female senior consultant

HEWITT

at a glance

Year Founded:	1940
Headquarters:	Lincolnshire, IL
1998 Revenues:	$858 million
Key Players:	Dale Gifford, Chief Executive Officer
Number of Consultants:	9,700
Web Page:	www.hewittassoc.com
Recruiting Contact:	Total Benefits Administration (TBA) Entry Recruiting
Address:	100 Half Day Road Lincolnshire, IL 60069
Fax, E-mail:	Fx: 847-295-0679 E-mail: careers@hewitt.com

About the Firm

Founded in 1940, Hewitt is one of the largest human resources services firms in the world. Its focus is in North America, where the firm has 30 offices, but has a global reach with 14 offices in Europe, 3 in Asia/Pacific, and in Latin America. Hewitt's angle of "improving business results through people" reminds you of a strategy firm. The firm has recently been running advertisements of empty football stadiums and concert halls to get the "people" message across.

Hewitt recently made *Forbes* magazine's "Top 500 Private Companies" and ranked sixth in *PC Week's* "Fast-Track 500" listing of the most innovative adopters of technology. The firm also has an enviable reputation as a quality place to work: In Kennedy Information's 1998 MBA study, Hewitt ranked #1 out of 59 firms in the "quality of life" category. (It dropped a bit to rank 5th in 1999.) Hewitt has a business casual dress code — not the only firm that has one, but it's the first firm we've seen that put a paragraph about it on its Web site.

Services

Hewitt serves most industries, and in addition to HR (80% benefits/compensation) consulting, the firm has a large outsourcing practice: About half of its revenues are derived from the service line. Recently, the firm announced its 100th outsourcing client (J.C. Penney) and the opening of a fourth outsourcing center in Woodlands, Texas, a 77-acre site that is expected to create over 1,000 jobs.

Career Paths

Whatever your educational background, you join Hewitt as an "associate." The firm uses non-hierarchical titles in an attempt to make its organization "noncompetitive." There is also no set career path. For training, Hewitt allows its associates to learn at its Total Benefits Administration University. Most new associates attend a training program that lasts between four and nine weeks, and will continue to attend TBA U "throughout their careers."

Summer Program

Hewitt offers a summer program, with internships available as business analysts, programmer analysts, and actuarial consultants. It is geared to college students who have finished their junior year with a GPA over 3.0 and preferably a major in one of the following disciplines: accounting, actuarial science, computer science, economics, finance, information systems/science, math, statistics, or similar concentrations. The program starts in May and lasts until August. Start and stop dates are flexible and the intern is paid a "competitive" salary. The program runs only at the Lincolnshire, (IL), Rowayton (CT), and Newport Beach (CA) offices. Interested students can contact any office directly, or can e-mail information to the recruiting contacts.

Recruiting

Hewitt recruits at a wide range of schools (see chart on page 104), and visit dates can be found on its "On the Road" section of its Web site.

Compensation

Benefits include health benefits, a tuition reimbursement plan, matching gift plan, deferred compensation plan, a dependent care account, an associate assistance program, and a work/life resources plan. The firm ranked low in Kennedy Information's MBA study in regards to compensation, as human resource firms historically pay less than their strategy, operations management, and IT counterparts.

Office Locations
US Office Locations

Atlanta, GA	Independence, OH	Rowayton, CT
Boston, MA	Lincolnshire, IL	San Antonio, TX
Bridgewater, NJ	Milwaukee, WI	San Francisco, CA
Charlotte, NC	Minneapolis, MN	Scottsdale, AZ
Chicago, IL	New York, NY	St. Louis, MO
Cincinnati, OH	Newport Beach, CA	Tampa, FL
Cleveland, OH	Orlando, FL	Washington, DC
Dallas, TX	Philadelphia, PA	Woodlands, TX
Denver, CO	Phoenix, AZ	
Detroit, MI	Pittsburgh, PA	*(continued on page 105)*

On-Campus Recruiting

Schools from which the firm recruits

- Alfred University
- Alma College
- Atlanta University Center
- Arizona State University
- Auburn University
- Augustana College
- Aurora University
- Babson College
- Barat College
- Baylor University
- Benedictine University
- Berry College
- Blackburn College
- Bradley University
- Brigham Young University
- Bryn Mawr College
- California State University, Fullerton
- Carleton College
- College of New Jersey
- Concordia University
- Cornell University
- DePaul University
- Dickenson College
- Dominican University
- Drake University
- Duquesne University
- Eastern Illinois University
- Elmhurst College
- Eureka College
- Fairfield University
- Florida A & M University
- Florida State
- Franklin & Marshall College
- Georgia State
- Georgia Tech
- Greenville College
- Grinnell College
- Haverford College
- Hope College
- Illinois College
- ISCPA
- Illinois State University
- Illinois Wesleyan University
- Indiana University
- Iowa State University
- Judson College
- Kalamazoo College
- Kenyon College
- Knox College
- Lake Forest College
- Lehigh University
- Lewis University
- Louisiana State University
- McKendree College
- MacMurray College
- Marquette University
- Miami University (Ohio)
- Michigan State University
- Millikin University
- Monmouth College
- North Central College
- Northern Illinois University
- North Park University
- Northwestern University
- Northwestern U. (Kellogg)
- Oberlin College
- Ohio State University
- Ohio University
- Olivet Nazarene University
- Pennsylvania State
- Pamona College
- Principia College
- Providence College
- Quincy University
- Rice University
- Rockford College
- Rutgers University
- St. Louis University
- St. Mary's College
- St. Xavier University
- Southern Methodist University
- Southwestern University
- Stanford GSB
- Stephen F. Austin
- Stetson University
- Texas A&M University
- Texas Tech University
- Trinity Christian College
- Trinity International University
- Trinity University, San Antonio TX
- Tulane University
- Union College
- University of Alabama
- University of California, Irvine
- UCLA
- University of California, San Diego
- University of California, Santa Barbara
- University of Central Florida
- University of Connecticut
- University of Florida
- University of Georgia
- University of Illinois
- University of Iowa
- University of Michigan
- University of Minnesota (Twin Cities)
- University of Northern Iowa
- University of Notre Dame
- University of Oklahoma
- University of Francis
- University of Texas—Business
- University of Virginia
- University of Wisconsin, Madison
- University of Wisconsin, Oshkosh
- Vassar College
- Virginia Tech
- Washington University
- Washington & Lee University
- Western Michigan University
- Wheaton College
- Yale University

Source: Hewitt and Kennedy Information/Consultants News

Non-US Office Locations (continued)

Amsterdam, The Netherlands	Mumbai, India
Bangalore, India	New Delhi, India
Bangkok, Thailand	Paris, France
Beijing, China	Pasig City, Phillipines
Brussels, Belgium	Peseux, Switzerland
Buenos Aires, Argentina	Prague, Czech Republic
Calgary, Canada	Rotterdam, The Netherlands
Caracas, Venezuela	Santiago, Chile
Col. Del Valle, Mexico	Sao Paulo, Brazil
Cologno Monzese, Italy	Shanghai, China
Dublin, Ireland	Singapore
Eindhoven, The Netherlands	Sydney, Australia
Geneva, Switzerland	Tokyo, Japan
Hato Rey, Puerto Rico	Toronto, Canada
Hertfordshire, UK	Utrecht, The Netherlands
Hong Kong	Vancouver, Canada
Jakarta, Indonesia	Vienna, Austria
Kuala Lumpur, Malaysia	Warsaw, Poland
Ljubljana, Slovenia	Wellington, New Zealand
Madrid, Spain	Wiesbaden, Germany
Melbourne, Australia	Zurich, Switzerland
Montreal, Canada	

Firm Evaluations

MBA Perceptions of Hewitt (*1-5 scale; 1=poor, 5=outstanding*)

	Prestige/ Reputation	Compensation	Long-Term Career Opportunities	Quality of Life
1999 Rating	**	**	**	*****

Source: Kennedy Information Research Group's 1999 MBA Recruiting Study

Leadership Notes

Dale Gifford has been the CEO of the firm since 1992. It says something about the firm's turnover considering Hewitt has had only three CEOs (including Gifford) since it was founded in 1940. Gifford joined the firm's actuarial service in 1972 and became Hewitt's manager of the compensation and benefits consulting business in 1982. Gifford is known in consulting circles as "the eternal optimist"; his one wish is that more people would look at their cup as being half full, rather than half empty.

IBM CONSULTING GROUP

at a glance

Year Founded:	1991
Headquarters:	White Plains, NY
1998 Consulting Revenues:	$990 million*
Key Players:	N/A
Number of Consultants:	5,000
Web Page:	www.consult.ibm.com
Resume Submission:	ibmusa@us.ibm.com
Address:	1133 Westchester Ave White Plains, NY 10604
Phone:	914-642-3000

*IBM's Global Services group is approximately $29 billion, but includes many non-consulting related services; IBM Consulting has recently been folded into the IBM Global Services Group.

About the Firm

IBM Consulting Group (IBM) was created in 1991 when IBM wanted to cash in on the consulting craze with its own group of experts and its own impressive brand power. The group has effectively leveraged IBM's enormous R&D efforts and is positioning itself as the lever between emerging technologies and business needs. The firm maintains a presence in 33 countries and has a high profile in the knowledge management area.

Services

IBM Consulting is big in information technology and operations management. It serves most industries but is especially strong in manufacturing, communications, and financial services. Consulting services include systems integration/application development, solutions consulting, and transformation consulting. The firm has made a concerted effort to develop a consulting approach where IT systems needs are driven by business choices. The firm has outgrown its early reputation as "plumbers" and has become recognized as credible management consultants.

Career Paths

Typically, MBAs join as associate consultants, and move to consultant within a year and a half. Usually, in another year and a half, one becomes a senior consultant. Industry-specific hires go into one of the service lines, while new MBAs are brought into the National Industry Support practice, where they work for four months to a year and later are "tagged" to specific industries. IBM is known for continuing education programs, as well as offering a foundation class to develop professional consultants. In order to become a consultant at IBM, you need to complete a certain number of engagements and meet specific requirements that a board reviews.

Another training tactic is to "team up people with MBAs to people with industry knowledge" on projects. IBM also has a mentoring program, even if you already have years of industry experience. All that might be missing in the initial training program is "more actual case studies and problem solving exercises."

Compensation

IBM consultants describe their compensation as "very competitive" or "really good." One consultant tried to benchmark his compensation against other IT consulting firms and "found it was above average." Another consultant was happy with IBM's initial offer and "accepted it on the spot." The firm gives "appreciable" signing bonuses, and provides an end-of-the-year bonus, as well as a "real good" benefits packages.

Office Life

The culture at IBM is more diverse than you might think. There aren't any "cloned MBAs" at the firm. The firm embraces teamwork, and it is "taken for granted" that you can "call someone you never heard of and ask for advice, while helping others you don't know." Despite all this teamwork, there is opportunity for "individual achievement" but if you "want your name in lights" you may be better off elsewhere. It's also "not a culture where people are stuck up and hard to be with." Most of the consultants are "driven people who are very successful," and the ideal consultant would probably be someone who is "inquisitive, curious, academic, and intellectual."

Hours on projects get heavy "at the beginning and the end" of the engagement, while the amount of hours you work "depends on your personality." One consultant mentioned that management "doesn't bug you to work long hours, they just want the client to be happy." (Note IBM's high quality of life ranking in the Kennedy Information survey.) Another perk about the firm is that IBM Consulting Group employees can take advantage of all IBM offices. If you're on a project in another city, you can work at any IBM location, which "is like a hotel" in that you sign up for an open workspace and are checked in. One thing to look out for is that you "don't become just another face" at such a huge company.

Geographic Locations

IBM Consulting Group allows its consultants to work out of any IBM office around the world. From a travel/lifestyle standpoint, this can be advantageous. Call the White Plains headquarters to find the offices closest to you.

Firm Evaluations

MBA Perceptions of IBM Consulting Group (*1-5 scale; 1=poor, 5=outstanding*)

	Prestige/ Reputation	Compensation	Long-Term Career Opportunities	Quality of Life
1999 Rating	***	***	****	*****

Source: Kennedy Information Research Group's 1999 MBA Recruiting Study

Comments from MBA Students About IBM Consulting Group

Culture	Like	Dislike
"Global"	"Structured career"	"Less strategic"
"Collegial, team-oriented"	"International exposure"	"Lack of consistency"
"Conservative"	"Many different opportunities"	"The amount of technical work"
"Large yet collegial"	"Focus on implementation"	"Poorly organized"
"Technical, broad scope"	"Very smart people"	"Bureaucracy of IBM Corp."
"New, disparate"		

Leadership Notes

Joseph Movizzo retired as IBM Consulting's world group general manager in January, 1998. Paul Lewis — IBM Consulting's former general manager, Asia Pacific Group — replaced him but recently stepped down following the reorganization.

Conclusion

Question: If there were any advice you'd give to a new hire going into IBM, what would it be?'

"The company really values people who can be thought leaders. It's a big organization, but you can't be expected to think with the pack."

— 33-year-old male consultant

"Consulting is a hard field to come up to speed on. You need to know a lot of different things. Learn as much as you can from the different people, and just know that it will take time to be an active member in the consulting community."

— male senior consultant

KPMG

at a glance

Year Founded:	1987
Headquarters:	New York, New York
1998 Consulting Revenues	$3.0 billion
Key Players:	Colin Sharman, Chairman
	Paul Reilly, International CEO
	James McGuire, International Managing Partner, Consulting Practice
Number of Consultants:	14,094
Web Page:	www.kpmg.com
Recruiting Contact:	Recruiting Coordinator
Address:	65 East 55th St.
	New York, NY 10022
Phone:	212-909-5000

About the Firm

KPMG — which stands for Klynveld, Peat, Marwick, and Goerdele, the firm's founding partners — is an internationally recognized professional services firm, though it was the last of the Big Five to initiate a global branding strategy.

KPMG has achieved impressive growth over the years, but certainly has its share of interesting stories. In Fall 1997, the firm was involved in merger talks with Ernst & Young that collapsed a few months later. The firm has tangled (three times) with boutique consulting firm Stern Stewart over ownership of "Economic Value Added" techniques. Most recently, in January 1998 KPMG alleged Stern Stewart was "bullying" speakers and attendees not to attend a KPMG EVA conference.

The firm hit a setback in early 1997 when national managing partner for strategic services Ted Fernandez wanted KPMG to take its consulting arm public. When the firm turned down this idea, Fernandez, Allan Frank, David Dungan, and Ulysses Knotts bolted to form Miami-based strategic consulting firm AnswerThink, which went public in May 1998. Over a dozen other KPMG partners followed Fernandez to AnswerThink.

Interestingly, today, KPMG is the only one of the Big Five — visibly, at least — pondering an IPO. The firm is currently waiting for a ruling on its IPO plan from the Independence Standards Board. Also, Cisco Systems Inc. invested $1 billion (a 19.9% stake) in KPMG LLP, the U.S. member firm of KPMG International. KPMG says it will use the cash infusion to hire 4,000 engineers and service professionals over the next 18 months to develop Internet-based services for clients.

In 1998, KPMG sold its Northeast Benefits Practice to Watson Wyatt, launched a global branding campaign ("It's Time for Clarity"), and saw its French practice defect to CSC. (A CSC consultant joked with *Consultants News*: "We scooped 'em right up!") Regardless, the firm enjoyed global consulting growth in 1998 of 30% worldwide. KPMG's marketers deserve credit for their eye-catching ads seen in *The Wall Street Journal* – playing off the fact that the average age of the firm's consultants is higher than that of most of its competitors.

Services

KPMG is strong in information technology and operations management consulting services. The firm offers five primary services: 1) strategy, 2) operations improvement, 3) package implementation, 4) systems integration and 5) outsourcing. It also has a human resources practice. KPMG is global and serves most industries.

Practice Line	Services	Practice Line	Services
Strategy	Business Strategy Transformation Planning Phase	*Package Solutions*	SAP, Baan, Oracle, PeopleSoft, others
Operations	Finance, HR, Customer Value Management, Product Fulfillment, IT, BPR, Risk, Activity Based, Change, and Project Management	*Systems Integration*	Knowledge Management, Electronic Commerce, Y2K, Enterprise Integration Services, Enterprise Networks, Data Warehousing, Custom Development, Systems Architecture
Outsourcing	Finance, HR, Document Management		

Source: KPMG and Kennedy Information/Consultants News

Summer Program

The firm has both summer and internship programs. Contact KPMG via its recruiting office, local office, or Web page to find out about available opportunities.

Recruiting

KPMG recruits widely at many first-and second-tier colleges. The firm also has a Web site completely devoted to recruiting aimed at college students interested in

KPMG careers. The site's address is www.kpmgcampus.com, and you can search for work by industry and/or area of study. A schedule of the firm's seminars and informational events can be found on the KPMG homepage.

Compensation

The firm is at or around the industry standard of $90,000 for new MBAs. Undergraduate salary information was not available.

Office Life

KPMG has a program called LifeWorks to deal with work/life balance issues. It has a child care program, a personal assistance counseling program, and an adoption program. These programs appear to pay dividends. The firm revels in its recognition by *Working Mother* magazine as one of the 100 best companies for working mothers. [The five categories *WM* uses to evaluate the organizations are wages, opportunity for women to advance, child care support, job flexibility, and family friendly benefits.] *Computerworld* magazine also listed KPMG as one of the "100 best places to work" in 1997.

There is a "good work ethic" at KPMG, and relations with management were described as "trustful and non-hierarchical." "The people" are often described as the one of the best things about the firm. A lack of training was a problem mentioned by a few.

Geographic Locations

KPMG operates in 840 cities around the world. Major US offices are listed below.

Major US Offices

Albany, NY	Denver, CO	Los Angeles, CA	Phoenix, AZ
Albuquerque, NM	Des Moines, IA	Louisville, KY	Portland, ME
Atlanta, GA	Detroit, MI	Memphis, TN	Providence, RI
Baltimore, MD	Fort Worth, TX	Miami, FL	Raleigh, NC
Baton Rouge, LA	Hartford, CT	Milwaukee, WI	Rochester, NY
Birmingham, AL	Houston, TX	Minneapolis, MN	Salt Lake City, UT
Boston, MA	Indianapolis, IN	Nashville, TN	San Antonio, TX
Burlington, VT	Jackson, MS	New York, NY	San Francisco, CA
Charlotte, NC	Kansas City, KS	Norfolk, VA	Seattle, WA
Chicago, IL	Las Vegas, NV	Oklahoma City, OK	Tulsa, OK
Cincinnati, OH	Lincoln, MA	Orlando, FL	Washington, DC
Dallas, TX	Little Rock, AR	Philadelphia, PA	Wichita, KS

Firm Evaluations

MBA Perceptions of KPMG (*1-5 scale; 1=poor, 5=outstanding*)

	Prestige/ Reputation	Compensation	Long-Term Career Opportunities	Quality of Life
1999 Rating	****	****	****	***

Source: Kennedy Information Research Group's 1999 MBA Recruiting Study

Comments from MBA Students About KPMG Peat Marwick

Culture:	*Likes:*	*Dislikes:*
"Revenue-driven"	"Meritocracy"	"People development"
"Dynamic, innovative"	"Teamwork"	"Cookie-cutter approach"
"Big, growing"	"Growth potential"	"Stuffy"
"Nurturing and respectful"	"Strong international presence"	"Volume business focus"
"Stress on teamwork, uncompetitive"	"Cross-functional mobility"	"Lack of best practices"

Leadership Notes

Jon C. Madonna was KPMG's CEO and chairman before being succeeded (in the chairman role) by Colin Sharman in January 1997. Sharman still maintains the position of senior partner at KPMG's UK practice. In June 1998, Paul Reilly, who was vice chairman for KPMG's financial services line, was elected the first international CEO of KPMG. At the same time, James B. McGuire, who was chairman for KPMG's consulting practice, was made the international managing partner for KPMG's global management consulting practice — a new position.

Conclusion

KPMG's consulting practice is growing far faster than its audit and tax advisory services and is seeking to make an imprint on the market with a new global branding strategy and the splitting off of its consulting arm — the first of the Big Five to do so. The firm has strong legs to stand on, including its strong reputation with women, minority advancement and work-life balance. Watch KPMG closely to see how its impending IPO plays in the marketplace.

MCKINSEY & COMPANY

at a glance

Year Founded:	1930
Headquarters:	New York, NY
1998 Consulting Revenues:	$2.5 billion
Key Players:	Rajat Gupta, Managing Director
Number of Consultants:	5,184
Web Page:	www.mckinsey.com
Recruiting Contact:	Recruiting Administrator, McKinsey & Company, Inc.
Address:	55 East 52nd St. New York, NY 10022
Phone, Fax, E-mail:	Ph: 212-446-7230, Fx: 212-688-5112 E-mail: career_opportunities@mckinsey.com

About the Firm

Does McKinsey & Co. actually need an introduction? You'd be hard-pressed to find any description of McKinsey in the media that doesn't have the words "preeminent" and "prestigious" in the description ("mystique" is also popular). McKinsey is the godfather of consulting firms, the "classic" strategy firm that carries considerable influence throughout the world. The firm was founded in 1930 and currently has over 4,000 consultants in 75 offices in 39 countries. Approximately 60% of its revenues are derived outside of the US, highlighting that McKinsey is a genuine global player.

The firm isn't known as a pioneer of ideas, despite heavy spending in R&D, but like Microsoft in technology, it doesn't have to be. To date, the firm has not advertised, sponsored golf tournaments, or made any of the high-profile "branding" efforts that many of the other large firms have. Nevertheless, along with Andersen Consulting, McKinsey is the most well-known brand name in the business.

Services

McKinsey has always been synonymous with strategy. The firm works mostly with CEOs and divisional presidents. "Nobody ever got fired for hiring McKinsey," goes the saying among senior managers at *Fortune* 500 companies. The firm tends to work with the world's largest international corporations, which undoubtedly have the biggest budgets for consulting projects. Though strategy is McKinsey's specialty, the firm derives considerable revenues from operations and IT-oriented consulting, which in 1998 were approximately $750 million and $500 million, respectively. The firm reportedly hired droves of IT consultants in 1997 and 1998, and continues to beef up its IT practice.

Career Paths

MBAs join as associates, and undergrads join as business analysts. After two years in an analyst role, assuming they prove they have ability, analysts are working at the same level as new associates. As far as the flexibility in career paths that other firms boast about, McKinsey does it the old-fashioned way. "Up or out is pretty much a fixture at McKinsey," says Stuart Flack, a PR representative at the firm. Up means engagement manager and, ultimately, partner. Out means taking advantage of McKinsey's unmatched alumni network — not a bad consolation prize.

Training

The firm has a formal national orientation and training program that lasts between two and seven days; consultants say this program is "effective." Formal, ongoing, firmwide training happens once or twice a year and involves seven to fourteen days. "Informal daily training," which takes the form of "coaching by engagement managers and peer associates," is considered the "most effective."

Summer Program

McKinsey has both summer and winter associate programs for MBAs. Programs lasts for 10 to 12 weeks and allow associates to participate as actual consultants on project teams. Feedback is provided by fellow team members and "others in the office." The firm didn't disclose exact figures, but says "most" summer associates are invited to return to the firm when their academic commitment is complete.

Recruiting

McKinsey is known to recruit among the top schools (and among the top 5% of classes). Stanford, Harvard, Tuck, Northwestern, and Wharton are primary target campuses. The firm is in an enviable position when it comes to hiring; "everyone wants to work at McKinsey," so the best-of-the-best mentality follows McKinsey's recruiters on campus. McKinsey actually hires 80% of the people it makes offers to, double the percentage of most firms (according to Kennedy Information Research Group survey findings).

Compensation

McKinsey is known for paying high salaries — the firm ranked number one out of 59 firms in terms of compensation in KI's 1998 and 1999 MBA survey. One consultant described his compensation as "very good" and — in traditional McKinsey style — refused to go into further detail. MBAs typically start at $90,000 to over $100,000, while undergrads are estimated to earn $45,000 or higher. An engagement manager three years out of business school would typically earn around $150,000 in salary plus bonus.

Office Life

McKinsey's "elite" culture is "intense, collegial, and client focused" and may be "stiff but bright." There is the feeling of being among "great people" and being involved in the "intellectual power" that is "The Firm." You can feel like you're working on something "that really made a positive difference." But it is a "competitive culture" as well. If you want to be "given lots of responsibility" and a "variety of challenges," and can handle the heavy travel and "incredible" working hours, this could be your firm.

In black and white on a glossy careers brochure — the equivalent of a warning label on a pack of cigarettes — the firm explains that the lifestyle of an undergrad business analyst can mean an average of 60 hours a week. Of course, the firm could say you'd have to work 23 hours a day, seven days a week and only sleep on plane rides and in elevators, and it'd still receive thousands of resumes each year.

Geographic Locations

US Locations	Non-US Locations		
Atlanta, GA	Amsterdam, The Netherlands	Istanbul, Turkey	Santiago, Chile
Bedminster, NJ		Jakarta, Indonesia	Sao Paulo, Brazil
Boston, MA	Bangkok, Thailand	Johannesburg, South Africa	Seoul, South Korea
Charlotte, NC	Barcelona, Spain		Shanghai, China
Chicago, IL	Beijing, China	Kuala Lumpur, Malaysia	Singapore
Cleveland, OH	Berlin, Germany		Stockholm, Sweden
Costa Mesa, CA	Bogota, Columbia	Lisbon, Portugal	Stuttgart, Germany
Dallas, TX	Brussels, Belgium	London, UK	Sydney, Australia
Detroit, MI	Budapest, Hungary	Madrid, Spain	Taipei, Taiwan
Houston, TX	Buenos Aires, Argentina	Melbourne, Australia	Tokyo, Japan
Los Angeles, CA	Caracas, Venezuela	Mexico City, Mexico	Toronto, Canada
Miami, FL	Cologne, Germany	Milan, Italy	Vienna, Austria
Minneapolis, MN	Copenhagen, Denmark	Montreal, Canada	Warsaw, Poland
Monterrey, CA	Delhi, India	Moscow, Russia	Zurich, Switzerland
New York, NY	Dublin, Ireland	Mumbai, India	
Pittsburgh, PA	Dusseldorf, Germany	Munich, Germany	
San Francisco, CA	Frankfurt, Germany	Osaka, Japan	
Seattle, WA	Geneva, Switzerland	Oslo, Norway	
Stamford, CT	Gothenburg, Sweden	Paris, France	
Washington, DC	Hamburg, Germany	Prague, Czech Republic	
	Helsinki, Finland		
	Hong Kong	Rome, Italy	

Firm Evaluations

Some consultants at McKinsey dislike the "over-structured approach to problem solving," but the main complaints are (typically) lifestyle-based, with some decrying the "unbelievable hours" and "very demanding" environment, with "too many weekends worked." (Note McKinsey's poor MBA ranking for quality of life.) Consultants also bemoan "inflexibility of interoffice transfers" and "ill-defined coaching/testing for professional development."

MBA Perceptions of McKinsey (*1-5 scale; 1=poor, 5=outstanding*)

	Prestige/ Reputation	Compensation	Long-Term Career Opportunities	Quality of Life
1999 Rating	*****	*****	*****	*

Source: Kennedy Information Research Group's 1999 MBA Recruiting Study

Comments from MBA Students About McKinsey & Company

Culture:	Likes:	Dislikes:
"Conservative"	"Vast amount of knowledge"	"Male-oriented"
"Hierarchical, professional"	"Amazing resources"	"Pressure, hours"
"Driven"	"Quality people, strong ethics"	"Arrogant"
"Aggressive, competitive"	"Quality of clients"	"Up or out policy"
"Global"	"Very prestigious"	
"Smart, excellent"	"Dynamic overseas opportunity"	

Leadership Notes

Rajat Gupta, who succeeded Fred Gluck, has the distinction of being the first non-western managing director of McKinsey & Co. Gupta was born in Calcutta, India, and moved to Delhi when he was five. After studying mechanical engineering at the Indian Institute of Technology, Gupta went on to get his MBA at Harvard Business School. He managed the Scandinavian office from 1982 to 1987, and became the Chicago office manager in 1989. He was elected to managing partner at age 45 in 1994 and was elected to a second term in 1997.

Conclusion

Make no mistake, McKinsey does embody many things that people hate about the consultant lifestyle: hard work, hard travel, hard hours, and hard career paths. But it is also where many of the best consultants go to work. In its marketing literature and on its Web page, the firm sensibly asks: "Is it right for you?" and alludes to the reality of its demanding business. But the opportunity to work at the most prestigious firm, get richly compensated, serve blue-chip clients, and become part of one of the world's great alumni networks is very alluring. McKinsey wins the majority of the job offers it makes: Few who are chosen turn down "The Firm." Beyond the prestige of market leadership, McKinsey is a safe career choice whether you want to make partner or spin out into industry. A smaller, faster growing boutique may offer quicker management responsibility, and a publicly-owned firm's stock options *might* make you rich quicker, but McKinsey remains a very compelling proposition.

Question: If there were any advice you would give to a new hire going into McKinsey, what would it be?

"Three things: Obligation to dissent; ask, ask, ask; and take initiative and responsibility."

— 27-year-old male associate

MERCER MANAGEMENT CONSULTING

at a glance

Year Founded:	1990
Headquarters:	New York, NY
1998 Consulting Revenues:	$255 million ($1.5 billion for all Mercer Consulting Group)
Key Players:	Jim Down, Co-chairman James Quella, Co-chairman
Number of Consultants:	Approximately 1,200 (11,304 for all Mercer Consulting Group)
Web Page:	www.mercermc.com
Recruiting Contacts:	Dana Crube (MBA) Amy Pate (Undergrad)
Address:	2300 N. Street N.W. Washington, D.C. 20037
Phone, Fax, E-mail:	Ph: 202-778-7560, Fx: 202-293-1371 E-mail: recruiting@mercermc.com

About the Firm

Mercer Management Consulting (MMC) was formed in 1990 with the acquisition of Strategic Planning Associates (a BCG spinoff) and Temple, Barker, and Sloane, two strategy consulting firms. In 1997, MMC also acquired Corporate Decisions. The firm is a member of Mercer Consulting Group, which is the umbrella organization of MMC, William M. Mercer, Lippincott & Margulies, and National Economic Research Associates. MMC prides itself on strategy consulting with a focus on growth strategies. Books published by MMC consultants such as *The Profit Zone* and *Profit Patterns* contribute to that focus (not to mention bolster the firm's branding and intellectual capital). Other books published in the past few years include *Value Migration* and *Grow to Be Great*. The firm also publishes *Mercer Management Journal*, a periodical somewhat similar to *The McKinsey Quarterly*.

Services

MMC focuses on strategy and operations management. In conjunction with the themes of most of its books, MMC focuses mostly on growth strategies. MMC "harnesses its thought leadership in three areas: Strategic Anticipation®, Business Design, and Value Growth Realization."

Career Paths

"If you are a superstar, they will promote you as soon as you can prove yourself capable," says one consultant. A MMC phrase is to gauge a consultant's progress based on "speedometer not odometer" (i.e., based on ability more than time served). Employees have reviews every six months. New hires straight out of an undergraduate school start as analysts, and the earliest you can become a consultant is about fourteen months. "15 months is a quick track, a year and a half is average." A new hire can be promoted through to the post-MBA position as an associate. As early as two years and three months into service, a BA-level hire could receive the post-MBA salary and title. "You don't have to be booted out to go back to business school. It's your choice. It's great flexibility."

For an undergraduate hire, the time from analyst to associate is more typically two to five years. MBAs start as associates, and the time from associate to principal ranges from three to six years (principal is first of two partner levels).

Training

At MMC, there is an initial training period of two weeks, which covers the basic methodologies, software applications, and learning what tools are available. After training, you're put on a case, and then "go back into a case simulation" which is an "excellent" simulated client case that "all of the new hires" from different offices work on. Once a year has passed, you move to "developing professional training, where people who have been there for a while talk with you." The training process is "not perfect, but there are good thoughts put into it, and it is a good use of time." A new hire feels like "someone who the firm wants to invest in" but "the majority of the training takes place on the project."

Summer Program

MMC's summer program allows the summer associates (SAs) to work on case teams, attend two training programs, and "interact with the firm's leaders and their peers." Every SA is assigned to a junior member at the firm for everyday questions, and a senior-level advisor who monitors the SA and provides feedback. MMC is proud of its program, and rightfully so: Almost three out of four BA/BS summer associates who were offered full-time positions at the firm accepted in 1998.

Summer Associate Data

Percent of 1998 BA/BS summer associates who were offered full-time positions:	80%
Percent of offers made that were accepted:	75%
Percent of 1998 MBA summer associates who were offered full-time positions:	85%
Percent of offers made that were accepted:	60%

Source: Mercer Management Consulting and Kennedy Information/Consultants News

Recruiting

MMC recruits at most of the top-tier business (and undergraduate) schools in the world. The firm has one of the best websites for students. Pick your school from a list and your student status (i.e. MBA, undergraduate) and the search engine will take you to the proper school page.

Number of Employees Hired, 1999

	Actual (*academic yr. ending: 6/1999*)	Summer Associates (*hired–1999*)
BA/BS	59	28
MBA	52	39
MA/PhD/Other Students	9	0

Source: Mercer Management Consulting and Kennedy Information/Consultants News

Compensation

Compensation at MMC is designed to "reward the superstars" and anyone who is "moving fast in the firm." Bonuses are also awarded and the percentages are "good, but not based on firm performance" because they are based primarily on the individual's work. Base salary varies, but is "right up there with everyone else." Said one consultant: "Compensation isn't going to get me to jump from Mercer to another firm." Also at MMC, "you don't hear people walking the halls, disgruntled about compensation."

Salary Data

	Average Starting Base Salary (1999)	Avg. Signing Bonus (1999)
BA/BS	$47,000	$5,000
MBA	$95,000	$20,000

Source: Mercer Management Consulting and Kennedy Information/Consultants News

Office Life

MMC's culture is "a combination between a boutique and a large firm" and the people are "a very comfortable group of people to be around" and are "incredibly intelligent and highly motivated." Like many firms, MMC tries to get all of its consultants back to the office on Fridays. Sometimes, case teams present the work they've done that week to everyone else in the office. "Strong" community service and social committees "bring the office together."

With the horizontal structure, an analyst may feel totally comfortable with "challenging a VP's thoughts as long as you can back yourself up." Some of the senior consultants "go out and drink with the junior staff." The lack of hierarchy is a "great thing about the firm" and there is "absolutely a lot of camaraderie in both the project teams and main office." Mercer is known to attract people who are "very social and a lot of fun." When you're working "crazy hours," having "some great people around can make a lot of difference."

MMC does a "pretty good job" at working with its employees to accommodate their needs outside of work, assuming you provide enough lead time. "If you look at a three-month project, and you see three weekends that you can't work, you can get them off." A consultant was put on an "interesting local case" when he said he didn't want to travel because of his wife's pregnancy. There are limits to what can be done, of course, because the firm is "very busy, to say the least," and there are many people who "have taken a month or two, or a year sabbatical to get away from it for a while, for personal reasons."

Geographic Locations

Major US Offices	Major Non US Offices
Boston, MA	Buenos Aires, Argentina
Chicago, IL	Hong Kong
Cleveland, OH	Lisbon, Portugal
New York, NY	London, UK
Pittsburgh, PA	Madrid, Spain
San Francisco, CA	Montreal, Canada
Washington DC	Munich, Germany
	Paris, France
	Toronto, Canada
	Zurich, Switzerland

Firm Evaluations

MBA Perceptions of Mercer (*1-5 scale; 1=poor, 5=outstanding*)

	Prestige/ Reputation	Compensation	Long-Term Career Opportunities	Quality of Life
1999 Rating	*****	*****	*****	***

Source: Kennedy Information Research Group's 1999 MBA Recruiting Study

Leadership Notes

Mercer Management Consulting split up its top job in April 1997 and named James Quella and Jim Down as vice chairmen. Quella and Down succeeded Thomas Waylett, who had been chairman since 1992. Waylett took his role in the first place when his successor, W. Walker Lewis, split to client Avon Products. Quella and Down report to Peter Coster, who is the president and "non-executive chairman."

Conclusion

Question: If there were any advice that you could give to a new hire or summer associate going into Mercer Management Consulting, what would it be?

"Take advantage of the wealth of knowledge that is around the firm. Don't get caught in the trap about thinking about your case issues and forgetting about other people. Talk to folks as much as possible; that's where the work gets really interesting."

— 30-year-old male senior associate

"Keep your eyes and ears open. There is such a significant amount to learn, so be careful not to get overwhelmed by it all."

— 23-year-old female analyst

"Be a team player. There is no magical formula. People who come to Mercer with their own agenda will not succeed, unlike someone who does whatever it takes to get the stuff done."

— 24-year-old male consultant

MITCHELL MADISON GROUP (MMG) (A USWEB/CKS COMPANY)*

at a glance

Year Founded:	MMG: 1994; USWeb/CKS: 1995
Headquarters:	MMG: New York, NY; USWeb: San Francisco, CA
1998 Revenues:	MMG: $257 million; USWeb/CKS: $229 million (total revenues)
Key Players:	Tom Steiner, President and COO, USWeb/CKS Robert Shaw, CEO, USWeb/CKS
Number of Consultants:	634 (MMG)
Web Page:	www.usweb.com
United States Recruiting Contacts:	Carol Labi, Recruiting Manager (graduate programs) Trisha Iglesias, Recruiting Coordinator (undergraduate)
Address (Mitchell Madison):	520 Madison Avenue New York, NY 10022
Phone, Fax, e-mail:	Ph: 212-372-9100, Fx: 212-372-4408 E-mail: recruiting@mmgnet.com

*Note: In December 1999, US Web/CKS merged with IT consulting firm Whittman-Hart

About the Firm

Now and again, a rock band out of nowhere will appear on the top 40 charts and rocket up the list, establish a reputation and make millions in sales. Mitchell Madison Group (MMG) was formed when it split off from A.T. Kearney a few years ago and rocketed to the *Consultants News'* Largest 40 list in 1997 with revenues of $100 million for 1996, which doubled the following year without a significant acquisition.

But as with some music sensations, they fall to earth, and with Mitchell Madison Group, it was a fast fall.

In 1994, on a street named Mitchell in upstate New York, ATK's financial services practice head Tom Steiner and other partners developed the plan to bolt from ATK. Steiner, along with 22 of the 25 founding partners of MMG, are ex-ATK and ex-McKinsey. Including the founding partners, Steiner took 135 consultants with him to form MMG, giving the start-up instant critical mass. The Manhattan address was on Madison Avenue, hence the name, Mitchell Madison Group. The firm now has 15 offices worldwide; 7 in North America, 6 in Europe, 1 in Africa, and 2 in Australia.

But disaster struck in early 1999, when the firm couldn't keep up with its own unbelievable growth. The firm began recruiting MBA's, undergrads, and industry experts faster than the firm could find work for them. The result? MMG was paying many consultants who were "beached" — as in hanging around the office like anxious firefighters waiting for the call — and thus not billable. The firm cut 7% to 10% of its consulting staff (typical of a firm in a cash crunch, according to *Consultants News*) and retained the investment bank Donaldson, Lufkin & Jenrette to help evaluate options. Rumors of a number of partners leaving the firm erupted around the same time as well. Among the partners known to have fled the firm included Will Riordan, who was a top recruiter at MMG and was described as "charismatic" by more than one consultant. Riordan is widely credited for making the firm a favorite on B-school campuses. The firm also rescinded — then reinstated — 15 offers made to undergraduates at six schools in the spring. It was widely believed MMG was up for sale.

On the morning of July 30th, 1999 Internet services firm USWeb/CKS announced its intent to acquire the firm. The deal has received favorable marks by some analysts. Part of the rationale for the acquisition of MMG by USWeb/CKS was MMG's financial services sector focus. The financial services industry is undergoing significant changes in the face of the e-commerce boom. The acquisition was also meant to bolster USWeb/CKS's presense in other regions of the world, including Asia, where MMG has a healthy business. (USWeb/CKS has experienced some fast growth itself, doubling its revenues in 1998.) At this point, it is unclear if USWeb/CKS intends to fold the MMG name to its own, but USWeb/CKS may still exploit the MMG name, which is almost synonymous with "strategy."

Services

MMG is a strategy and operations management firm with roots in the financial services sector. The firm has increased its activity in telecommunications/media, high tech, retail, pharmaceuticals, and automotive. USWeb/CKS specializes in providing "Internet technology and marketing communications" and services from "business process automation to e-commerce solutions," and is not industry-focused.

Career Paths

Graduates with no prior business experience enter MMG as business analysts. After a few years they are expected to advance to the associate level: The firm doesn't believe it has a "lockstep" career path, or an "up or out" mentality. MBAs arrive as associates (consultants) and can pursue the path from associate to manager to shareholder at "the pace they choose."

Training

At MMG, training starts with a few days of computer education and about a week to "figure out consultant stuff," with an ITC (Introduction To Consulting) program to follow. For non-MBA hires, there is a new "mini-MBA-like" training program for the Ph.D's, industry hires, or other non-traditional hires. One consultant described the training as "not as robust" as at some other firms, but didn't think it needed to be, explaining that "90% of what you learn is on the job."

Summer Program

MMG has a summer program that facilitates "tons of client contact" in the traditional hands-on manner. Training is brief, sometimes with "one day training and one day orientation." One summer associate remembers coming in on June 15th and being asked to get on a plane the next morning to go to a client site. The salary is "on the level of the major firms."

Recruiting

MMG seeks individuals who have "interesting hobbies" and a lot of creativity. The firm is "not aggressive like BCG, McKinsey and Bain" in its recruiting style, and the consensus is that it doesn't need to be any more aggressive. In fact, MMG will likely be less aggressive this recruiting season while the acquisition is completed and the two firms are fully integrated.

Compensation

MMG ranked an impressive 7th in MBA's perception of compensation among the top fifty firms in 1999. Compensation is described by the consultants as "competitive" and "fair." It will be interesting to see how the addition of stock options (now that MMG is part of a publicly traded company) will affect compensation.

Office Life

The business analysts at MMG "set the tone of the firm." The people are young "and really interesting." However, it can be "a bit crazy at times." There are many "cowboys" but the consultant who said that meant it in a "positive" manner. There isn't a single personality that drives the firm, and some people "work seven days a week" while others protect their weekends. There is "creative tension" resulting from the mixed personalities at the firm. Your hours may not be bad as long as you understand they'll "vary tremendously."

In the New York office, "the white American man is the minority" and women are "well represented" with a handful at the partner level. At all of the offices, "you'll find names that come from all over the world." Another said MMG is "a very diverse group" and "if you're male and pale, you're in the minority." Like at most other consulting firms, this is not the case at the partner level.

MMG is known to "attract people who resist bureaucracy." One said "if you're conservative, straight-laced, and work in an environment that is very structured, this is not the firm for you." Young, entrepreneurial folks would probably be in their element here, as long as they can understand and put up with the occasional "chaos with administrative details" like "getting paper at the copier." With the impending acquisition, the chaos will likely be worse, but will also likely be temporary.

Geographic Locations (MMG)

Major U.S. Offices	Major Non U.S. Offices
Boston, MA	Frankfurt, Germany
Chicago, IL	London, UK
Los Angeles, CA	Madrid, Spain
New York, NY	Melbourne, Australia
San Francisco, CA	Montreal, Canada
	Munich, Germany
	Paris, France
	Sydney, Australia
	Toronto, Canada
	Zurich, Switzerland

Firm Evaluations

MBA Perceptions of Mitchell Madison Group (*1-5 scale; 1=poor, 5=outstanding*)

	Prestige/Reputation	Compensation	Long-Term Career Opportunities	Quality of Life
1999 Rating	*****	*****	*****	*****

Source: Kennedy Information Research Group's 1999 MBA Recruiting Study

Leadership Notes

Before helping found Mitchell Madison Group, Steiner was head of A.T. Kearney's financial services group for three years. Prior to that, he was one of the many folks recruited out of McKinsey to build up ATK's practice (Steiner himself was a McKinsey partner for ten years). Steiner was made president and COO of USWeb/CKS after the acquisition.

Robert Shaw, the CEO of USWeb/CKS, joined the firm in November 1998, and prior to his appointment, he was a member of Oracle Corp's executive team for six years. Shaw himself believes meshing the cultures of his firm with MMG's will be the most challenging part of the merger. We'll see if he's right.

Conclusion

Question: If there was any advice you could give to a new hire or a summer associate joining Mitchell Madison Group, what would it be?

"Be proactive, and since there are not many systems in place, it's your responsibility to just get out and get acquainted with people."

— 25 year old female summer associate

"Three things: One is be flexible, because the firm doesn't have all the policies and procedures other firms have. Two is take the ball, and run with it; the firm gives you enough rope to hang yourself or make your career. And three is just to be involved with helping to build the firm; there's lots of opportunity."

— 28 year old female consultant

"Find a good second year analyst and learn! They are the ones who always know what is going on. Get humble and learn."

— 38 year old male consultant

"Be yourself and things will work out for you. This firm expects people to be honest, open, and idiosyncratic. You'll be happier and more successful if you're yourself, and the firm allows you to be yourself."

— 29 year old male summer associate

MONITOR COMPANY

at a glance

Year Founded:	1983
Headquarters:	Cambridge, MA
1998 Consulting Revenues:	$225 million
Key Players:	Mark B. Fuller, Chairman and CEO
	Michael E. Porter, Harvard Business School
	Joe Fuller, Director
Number of Consultants:	850
Web Page:	www.monitor.com
Recruiting Contact:	Sandra Morris
Address:	25 First Street
	Cambridge, MA 02141
Phone, Fax:	Ph: 617-252-2501, Fx: 617-252-2114

Professional Breakdown

# Global Account Mgrs	55
# Women Global Account Mgrs	10
# Minority Global Account Mgrs	5
# Professionals	790
# Women Professionals (excl. partners)	235
# Minority Professionals (excl. partners)	115

Source: Monitor Company and Kennedy Information/Consultants News

About the Firm

Monitor Company was founded in 1983 when Harvard Business School professor Michael Porter and colleague Mark Fuller decided to parlay the success of Porter's best-seller *Competitive Strategy* into a consulting company. The firm took off quickly, and became a hot ticket on campus. By 1998, Monitor had $225 million in worldwide revenues, 25 offices, and 850 professionals.

While Porter is not active with the firm on a day-to-day basis, Monitor has a tradition of using his "methodologies" such as Five Forces and Value Chains, as well as Porter's work on the competitiveness of nations. In recent years, Monitor has built relationships with other academics, and this strong academic base remains a distinguishing characteristic of the firm, along with a view that the consultant's primary role should be as a teacher and facilitator.

Culturally, Monitor considers itself a meritocracy. While there are internal titles like Case Team Leader (CTL), the firm avoids formal hierarchies and titles. Power is concentrated at the large, Harvard-adjacent Cambridge head office, where all of the founders and most of the partners are based. Chairman and CEO Mark Fuller provides an intense, visionary style of leadership, frequently demolishing and rebuilding internal systems, while brother Joe brings home the bacon as the firm's top rainmaker. As the founders have moved into their forties, Monitor's loose but intense style has mellowed somewhat.

The firm has deliberately sought a low profile that some would call secretive. Among former big name clients: AT&T (which once paid Monitor over $50 million in a single year) and Sears (which didn't stick with Monitor's strategy of "Everyday Low Pricing").

In 1998, Monitor beefed up its financial strategy capabilities, seeing M&A advisory work and valuations as lucrative areas. It also raised a $500 million buy-out fund called Monitor Clipper Partners, hoping that its consultants will make the firm more money by improving the performance of acquired companies.

Services

Monitor doesn't pretend to be anything other than a generalist strategy firm. Its strategy work includes business unit development, competitive analysis/simulation, and nation-state advisory services. The firm has been historically strong in retail and telecommunications, but has no enduring industry practice areas. None of its consultants are expected to specialize by industry.

Career Paths

The firm doesn't encourage industry specialization, a model followed by many of the big strategy firms. Mark Fuller told *Consultants News* back in 1989: "What we sell is strategy, and the ability to liberate the industry expertise that the client has…our job is not to set up an industry expert to compete with (the client's) industry expert."

The career path is "highly individualized" but the expectation is to gain "substantial" management responsibilities as early as six months out. After starting as a consultant, you may become a case team leader after six months to two years. All promotions within the firm are "based on the individual with no average path." The loose structure at Monitor, which will be covered later in this profile, is one of the things that some of its consultants *love*. The freedom to choose how you want to plan your career and what you want to do at Monitor is very appealing to some. The lack of formal job titles makes it hard to map out a standard career progression.

The teaching side of the firm's work is also appealing. One consultant mentioned how much he liked the emphasis on teaching, that he was thrilled working on a team with a client and "brainstorming with the client and teaching him or her how to think strategically."

Training

Consultant training is "spread out" over the course of a consultant's tenure. Orientation is "a couple days, you learn about the firm philosophies." After orientation, you are generally "on your own."

Summer Program

Monitor has summer internship and summer consulting programs, the former being for undergrads who are about to complete their last year in college, and the latter for graduates of MBA and other higher education programs. In both cases, you're on a team as a "full-time" consultant. The programs are ten to twelve weeks in length and in addition to your work on a case team, you have opportunities to hang out with senior members of the firm and go to office parties and events with the rest of the staff. During the summer program, you have two mentors: a senior member of the firm who serves as an advisor for development, and an experienced consultant who'll point you in a direction if you have questions. Most feedback comes from members of your case team. You are expected to have "the willingness to learn, an inquisitive nature, and obviously [the qualities of] a team player."

Summer Associate Data

Percent of 1998 BA/BS summer associates who were offered full-time positions:	70%
Percent of offers made that were accepted:	75%
Percent of 1998 MBA summer associates who were offered full-time positions:	70%
Percent of offers made that were accepted:	66%

Source: Monitor Company and Kennedy Information/Consultants News

Recruiting

The firm recruits at more schools than are listed in the following chart, but given the close proximity to Harvard, it's no surprise that more recruits come from there than from any other school. Being smallish compared to the market giants, Monitor obviously hires fewer recruits, and can afford to be highly selective (not every summer associate was offered a full-time position).

Number of Employees Hired 1999-2000

	Actual (*academic yr. ending: 6/1999*)	Expected (*academic yr. ending: 6/2000*)	Summer Associates (*hired–1999*)
BA/BS	90	100	26
MBA	35	42	15
MA/PhD/other students	14	18	0
Industry Experts	2	4	0

Source: Monitor Company and Kennedy Information/Consultants News

On-Campus Recruiting

Schools from which the firm actively recruits (Note: Monitor also recruits elsewhere)	# of BA/BS recruits ('98)	# of MBA recruits ('98)
Harvard	10	6
University of Pennsylvania	8	3
Northwestern	N/A	1
Stanford	3	1
INSEAD	N/A	6

Source: Monitor Company and Kennedy Information/Consultants News

Compensation

Starting salaries match rivals BCG and Bain — around $90K for new MBAs. The firm also offers health coverage, long-term disability, life insurance, and vacation. The year-end performance bonus for all consultants at all levels is driven by the firm's and the individual's performance. It could exceed your salary or it could be zero. Unlike many other firms, it's possible for a star BA to make more than a newish MBA, due to Monitor's meritocratic pay philosophy. The firm is highly rated in perceived compensation in KI's study. MBAs describe compensation as "healthy" and "very competitive." Signing bonuses are the norm, and "if you do a summer [internship], they'll pay for your last year of school."

Office Life

There is "a ton" of camaraderie at the office. Monthly, the firm has functions outside the office that include soccer games and sometimes a BBQ at a case team leader's house. The firm "finds family important" and is flexible, "without a lot of emphasis on face time." The culture is meant "to be as meritocratic as possible" and the firm believes it has "the closest thing to a meritocracy in the strategy consulting business." There is "less structure here than at other consulting firms," so an individual would have to like that environment in order to enjoy his/her work. There "isn't a lot of hand holding" at the firm, so you have to be proactive about questions and training.

Monitor has somewhat of a reputation for long work hours (note the lower quality of life score on the MBA study). Fifty-five hours a week appears to be the mean, and "people do what it takes to get the job done." That notwithstanding, there is "no expectation you will put in a specific number of hours. How and where you get the job done is up to you."

Accordingly, your work-life balance is open to discussion and "you're expected to express your interests very clearly and the firm will do what it can to accommodate what you want to do." It fits in with the entrepreneurial and loose structure: You must be proactive to get what you want.

Geographic Locations

US Offices	Non US Offices and Branches	
Cambridge, MA	Sao Paulo, Brazil	Moscow, Russia
Los Angeles, CA	Amsterdam, The Netherlands	Athens, Greece
New York, NY	Frankfurt, Germany	Istanbul, Turkey
	London, UK	Tel Aviv, Israel
	Madrid, Spain	New Delhi, India
	Milan, Italy	Hong Kong
	Munich, Germany	Manila, The Philippines
	Paris, France	Seoul, South Korea
	Stockholm, Sweden	Tokyo, Japan
	Zurich, Switzerland	Singapore
	Johannesburg, South Africa	Toronto, Canada

Firm Evaluations

Monitor isn't for everyone, because "if you're a geek, you're not appealing" and "huge egos just won't work" at the firm. The people who are right for Monitor have been described as "more of a leader than a follower," and people who want to examine and be involved in "a range of experiences" across industries and practices. People who are "open to learning and very bright" will enjoy the firm, and if you "ran clubs in school, or started your own company, or created a volunteer organization," Monitor would be your kind of place. People who "tend to be very passionate about things" and "want to make the world a better place" will think of the firm as a second home.

MBA Perceptions of Monitor (*1-5 scale; 1=poor, 5=outstanding*)

	Prestige/ Reputation	Compensation	Long-Term Career Opportunities	Quality of Life
1999 Rating	*****	*****	*****	***

Source: Kennedy Information Research Group's 1999 MBA Recruiting Study

Leadership Notes

Mark Fuller was an associate professor at Harvard Business School, where Michael Porter continues teaching business strategy. Porter, who has authored over 15 books and 60 articles, began teaching at HBS in the early seventies, and Fuller began a few years later. Mark's brother, Joe, was recruited out of Bain & Company in 1983 and assisted them in founding Monitor Company. Some other "Bainies" followed, undoubtedly impressed by Fuller and Porter's vision.

Conclusion

Question: If there were any advice you could give to a new hire or summer associate going into Monitor Company, what would it be?

Be as open and honest about what you want to do so people can help you craft a career path that matches your passions. I think this is a place that gives you the opportunity to do all that. In a nutshell, be open, be honest."

— 30-year-old male consultant

"Test the fit. And make sure that you're okay without structure and that you're very open to learning. And it's okay to ask lots of questions."

— 27-year-old female summer associate

PRICEWATERHOUSECOOPERS

at a glance

Year Created:	1998
1998 Consulting Revenues	$6.0 billion
Key Players	Scott Hartz, Managing Partner, Global Consulting MC Services
	Lewis Krulwich, Senior Managing Partner Americas Theatre
	Dennis Dall, Senior Managing Partner, Asia/Pacific Theatre
	Vic Luck, Sr. Managing Partner, Europe, Middle East, Africa Theatre
	John Jacobs, Global Deputy Leader for Services
	Peter Davidson, Global Deputy Leader for Industry
Number of Professionals:	40,800
Web Page:	www.pwcglobal.com
MBA Recruiting Contact:	MBA Recruiting Team, Attn: Mary Ann Miniscalco
Address:	9399 W. Higgins Road. Suite 770 Rosemont, Il 60018
Phone:	847-685-4088

Partner & Professional Breakdown (for U.S. consulting activities only)

# Partners	647
# Women Partners	67
# Minority Partners	44
# Women Professionals (excl. partners)	4,156
# Minority Professionals (excl. partners)	2,830

Source: PwC and Kennedy Information/Consultants News

About the Firm

PricewaterhouseCoopers (PwC) is the newly-merged professional services firm created from Price Waterhouse and Coopers & Lybrand. The idea to merge was officially announced in mid-September 1997 after several months of speculation. It cleared all of the regulatory hurdles, plus most importantly was approved by enough of the firms' partners (one unnamed PW leader allegedly circulated a memo saying the firm wouldn't give an inch in its "acquisition" of C&L). The firms operated independently until July 1, 1998, barely a month after they disclosed the biggest mystery of all: the new name. At the cost of $1.6 million dollars (they hired a consultant) the firms created the PwC name, rejecting *Consultants News'* suggestion of naming the firm "§" which would've meant: "the firms formerly known as Price Waterhouse and Coopers & Lybrand."

Observers generally give PwC high marks for its smooth handling of a complex transition. Inevitably there have been a few mutterings, but so far this huge merger has gone well. Both firms have great name recognition in both the audit and consulting worlds, but we can't help feeling sorry for Lybrand.

Services
The Management Consulting Services (MCS) practice provides — in PwC terms — Strategic Change, Process Improvement, and Technology Solutions, focused in five key industries: 1) Financial Services; 2) Consumer and Industrial Products; 3) Information, Communications, and Entertainment; 4) Energy; and 5) Services. The MCS is also big in the implementation of enterprise resource planning systems such as SAP, PeopleSoft, and Oracle, with over 10,000 dedicated consultants.

Career Paths
PwC's MCS practice hires MBAs into its Strategic Change or Process Improvement areas. There are services within each of these areas that an MBA can choose to specialize in, within an industry or across industry.

Strategic Change is composed of:
1. Corporate Business Strategy
2. Operations Strategy
3. Organizational Strategy
4. Change Strategy
5. IT Strategy

Process Improvement is composed of:
1. Market and Customer Management
2. Supply Chain Management
3. Human Resource Management
4. Financial Cost Management
5. Information Technology Management
6. Industry Specific Process Improvement

MBA hires can either choose to be part of a cross-industry practice or part of an industry-focused area. They can expect to be promoted to principal consultant and then director before becoming a partner.

Training

After 2-3 months in the field, there is a week-long MBA training program, which focuses on learning/reviewing various analytical tools and methodologies, hearing presentations on what the different partners are focusing on, and meeting/networking with others.

For BA/BS hires, the firm provides an entry-level IT training program called MITIS — MCS Information Technology Individual Study (leave it to consultants to put an acronym in an acronym) — which provides "excellent hands on training." Consultants at all levels are "expected to pursue a lot of additional education." The firm recently opened a global training center in Tampa, FL at a cost of $52 million. An aerial photograph of the 23-acre center resembles a college campus. It has a four-story classroom building, "upscale suites" (dorm rooms!), and recreational facilities.

Summer Program

Internships for BA/BS students are limited to entry-level IT and research consultants. The Summer Intern Program for MBAs has students join the firm in the Strategic Change and Process Improvement consulting practices. The purpose, according to PwC, "is to let MBA students see our clients and staff and give them an understanding of our methodologies and approach to client situations. The summer intern program allows MBAs to utilize the skills they've learned thus far and apply their knowledge to our client engagements." The summer associates' responsibilities include compiling research, conducting market analysis, and assisting in the preparation of proposals and client presentations. During the summer, MBAs work closely with a partner who will mentor and coach them.

Summer Associate Data

Percent of 1998 BA/BS summer associates who were offered full-time positions:	70%
Percent of offers made that were accepted:	75%
Percent of 1998 MBA summer associates who were offered full-time positions:	70%
Percent of offers made that were accepted:	66%

Source: PwC and Kennedy Information/Consultants News

Recruiting

PwC claims to be recruiting about 1,000 consultants per month and also claims to be the largest recruiter of MBAs in the United States. One recruit said the firm "did a nice job wining and dining us and making us feel happy." A fruit basket and a PwC sweatshirt were also included in his recruiting experience. For folks who want to pursue employment at the firm, resumes can be sent in on-line or mailed to any recruiting director. A consultant who worked on the screening process had common-sense (but often overlooked) advice for students who want to enter the firm. "If you say the same thing on your resume to E&Y that you say to us, you won't get hired," he continues, "tell us why you're a fit for the firm, not why the firm is a fit for you." (See chart on page 139 for specific school recruiting information.)

Number of Employees Hired 1999-2000

	Actual (academic yr. ending: 6/1999)	Expected (academic yr. ending: 6/2000)	Summer Associates (hired–1999)
BA/BS	1100	1100	100
MBA	250	220	75

Source: PwC and Kennedy Information/Consultants News

Compensation

The MBA starting salary range is between $65,000 and $105,000, and the MBA signing bonus range is between $5,000 and $20,000. All new MBA hires are offered a $5,000 relocation allowance. For MBA summer interns, the firm offers second year tuition payment like many of the large firms. All new MBA and BA/BS hires have an incentive bonus plan. The firm also offers a number of graduate school scholarship options.

One consultant two years out of business school is "not overwhelmed" by his compensation and noted that anyone would be hard-pressed to find "a consultant who said they were overpaid." One complained that in the immediate aftermath of the merger things take a long time — such as his current appeal for a salary increase. The overriding attitude of consultants is that they still believe in the firm and are riding out the integration phase.

Salary Data

	Average Starting Base Salary (1999)	Avg. Signing Bonus (1999)
BA/BS	$46,000	$3,000
MBA	$95,000	$22,500

Source: PwC and Kennedy Information/Consultants News

On Campus Recruiting:

BA/BS Recruits ('98)

School	#	School	#
Barnard	4	U. of Southern California	8
Boston College	5	U. of Texas-Austin	37
Brown	4	University of Virginia	31
Bucknell	4	University of Wisconsin	6
Carnegie Mellon	8	Virginia Tech	30
Columbia	20	Washington University	11
Cornell	37	Wellesley	11
Dartmouth	8	William & Mary	20
Drexel	3	Yale	1
Duke University	10	**TOTAL (BA/BS)**	**658**
Florida State	15		
George Mason	1		
Georgetown U.	3		
Georgia Tech.	25		
Howard U.	5		
Indiana U.	24		
James Mason	19		
New York U.	10		
North Carolina St.	21		
Northwestern	4		
Pennsylvania St.	32		
Princeton	10		
Purdue	7		
Rice University	5		
RPI	4		
Rutgers University	5		
Southern Methodist	5		
Southern U.	1		
Stanford	9		
Texas A&M	15		
Trinity	5		
UC Berkeley	21		
UCLA	22		
University of Florida	17		
University of Arizona	16		
University of Chicago	5		
University of Colorado-Boulder	6		
U. of Illinois-Urbana	23		
University of Iowa	10		
University of Maryland	10		
University of Michigan	20		
University of Pennsylvania	13		
University of South Carolina	12		

MBA Recruits ('98)

School	#
Arizona State	8
Berkeley	2
Carnegie Mellon	9
Chicago	5
Columbia	16
Cornell	1
Darden	6
Duke	10
George Washington	5
Georgetown	6
Harvard	12
Howard U.	6
Indiana	9
Kellogg	17
Maryland	7
Michigan	23
Michigan State	1
MIT	6
NYU	17
Penn State	2
Texas	10
Tuck	5
UCLA	7
UNC Kenan	3
USC	6
VA Tech	1
Vanderbilt	4
Washington U.	4
Wharton	17
William & Mary	3
Yale SOM	4
TOTAL (MBA)	**270**

Source: PwC and Kennedy Information/Consultants News

Office Life

The merger didn't have a tremendous impact on the day-to-day rhythms of the firm. There is camaraderie around the office, especially reported by PW folks; on project teams, there is "forced camaraderie." Consultants are enthusiastic about the merged PwC because "now there are twice as many projects to work on." Another commented that there are "so many bright people with different areas of expertise and interests" in the firm that you can learn from and "ask any questions." Also, when one consultant sends out a request for help from another consultant, he/she often "gets more than what was requested," suggesting a healthy cooperative culture.

It's up to each consultant to create the balance between work and life because "it's pretty easy to let work take over." For the first phases of a project you can work "12 to 15 hours a day," but it can wane in the later stages. Despite it all, some consultants would "pull any of my friends in here." Resources such as concierge services are available to consultants, and the firm is trying to minimize the amount of Sunday night travel that has to occur and "insure that you will be home on Thursday evening." The type of consultant who would enjoy PwC would have to be on a "fast learning curve and possess technological aptitude," along with the ability to "appreciate change and unpredictability, no matter what the impact on personal or social life." PwC does have a six-months-of-unpaid-leave program for consultants who want to get away from the consulting life for a while.

Geographic Locations

PwC has about 800 offices around the world. Full integration of PW and C&L will most certainly result in the consolidation and closing of redundant offices, but the firm maintains a presence in most major cities.

What Don't They Like?

Post-merger stress with bureaucracy is a problem but "not too big a thorn" in a consultant's side. There is concern with the rapid growth last year, including fears that the firm was "becoming an Andersen!" and growing "too quick, too fast." Another source thinks a key focus should be retention because the firm is "putting too much emphasis on recruiting" and "not a great job at keeping people." In general, "most consultants complain about" lifestyle issues that are associated with most any consulting firm.

Firm Evaluations

MBA Perceptions of PwC (*1-5 scale; 1=poor, 5=outstanding*)

	Prestige/ Reputation	Compensation	Long-Term Career Opportunities	Quality of Life
1999 Rating	****	****	****	****

Source: Kennedy Information Research Group's 1999 MBA Recruiting Study

Comments from MBA Students About PricewaterhouseCoopers

Culture:	Likes:	Dislikes:
"Implementation-oriented"	"Diversity of work"	"Bureaucracy, growing pains"
"Relaxed and collegial"	"Advancement opportunity"	"Poor infrastructure (HR, training, etc.)"
"Structured, yet high growth"	"Good team spirit"	
"Decentralized, flexible"	"Friendly culture"	"Mentoring and resource planning"
"Hard work, team-oriented"	"Great people who don't take self too seriously"	"Impersonal due to large size"
"Bright, energetic"		"Too process-oriented"
"Global"		"Politics"

Leadership Notes

In terms of former affiliation, Price Waterhouse got the best seats in the house on the consulting side of the business; one Price Waterhouse partner told *Consultants News* "Price clearly won in terms of leadership positions." The chairman of the entire firm is Nicholas Moore, who was the former chairman of Coopers & Lybrand International. James J. Schiro, the PwC CEO, was formerly the CEO of Price Waterhouse. Neither man — both members of the American Institute of CPAs — came from the consulting side of the business. Scott Hartz, the global managing partner for PwC's management consulting services, is credited for helping Price Waterhouse convert into a global organization back in 1996.

Conclusion

Question: If you could give one piece of advice to a new hire or summer associate going into PwC, what would it be?

"If you're interviewing, prove your technical prowess and your leadership in technical prowess."

— 24-year-old male IT consultant

"One of the biggest things that makes people unhappy is when they are on a crappy project. Take the opportunity to figure out what you want to do and go do that."

— 29-year-old male manager

"Take the initiative to meet others and network. Be proactive in managing your own career within the firm."

— 27-year-old male associate

TOWERS PERRIN

at a glance

Year Founded:	1934
Headquarters:	New York, NY
1998 Revenues:	$1.2 billion
Key Players:	John Lynch, Chairman/Chief Executive Officer
Number of Consultants:	8,155
Web Page:	www.towers.com
Recruiting Contact:	Mary Giannini, National Campus Recruiting Manager
Address:	100 Summit Lake Drive Valhalla, NY 10595
Phone, Fax, e-mail:	Ph: 914-745-4258, Fx: 914-745-4621 E-mail: giannim@towers.com

About the Firm

Founded in 1934 as Towers, Perrin, Forster and Crosby, Towers Perrin (TP) is a giant in human resources consulting (approximately 65% of revenues are in benefits/compensation work). The firm has over 7,500 employees, yet TP likes to think it has a "small firm" environment, with all of the advantages of a global player. The firm has 82 offices in 75 cities and 27 countries. TP publishes 15 newsletter/magazine/executive briefs on issues ranging from investments and the pension fund industry in Canada (*AlfaBeta*) to international pay and benefit developments (*Worldwide Pay and Benefits Headlines*). It has several proprietary methodologies that it uses in its consulting practices. The firm maintains the National Employee Benefit Center (NEBC) to handle employee inquiries for its benefits administration practice. The firm has a favorable reputation, though was embarrassed in early 1997 when a *Wall Street Journal* article alleged the firm sold different major clients nearly identical reports. However, the effect on the firm's growth and success has been insignificant.

Services

The firm serves most industries through three service lines delivered by three distinct entities: 1) human resource and general management consulting (through Towers Perrin), 2) insurance industry and risk management consulting (through Tillinghast-Towers Perrin), and 3) reinsurance consulting (through Towers Perrin Reinsurance).

Career Paths

Undergrads are hired in as associates, then they "usually go back for their MBA." MBAs enter the firm as consultants, and can expect promotion to senior consultant after three to five years, with an additional two to four years after that to become partner. The length of time it takes to become a partner from the MBA level is "about five to eight years on the average."

Training

There is "very little" training at the start, with, in the firm's words, "client-focused work right after hiring." The firm provides a three-day orientation, but it is only given every six months. The firm does "prefer that you worked for a few months" before attending anyway. Orientation covers skills and the firm's network, among other things, and "there are some redundancies" if you have been with the firm for awhile. The consultants like that they can "meet people from all over the country" at the orientation. Nevertheless, most training is "on the job" and there are "always opportunities" for seminars and other types of education, but you have to be "proactive and make time for it."

Summer Program

1998 was the first year of the TP summer program; the firm's General Management Services has a formalized intern program for MBAs, which lasts 8 to 10 weeks and has students work as consultants. Interns are hired in all lines of business, and it will be interesting to see how the summer program measures up after it has been around for awhile.

Recruiting

TP expanded its list of B-schools in 1998 and has been "focusing more on its efforts to recruit on campus." One consultant who was recruited out of Columbia Business School thought the TP presentation was "one of the better ones" he saw during recruiting season. They "spoke about all areas of the practice" and of their experiences with the firm. This consultant was very impressed that the firm didn't want him to accept his offer until he came back to "meet with some consultants to go over what I plan to do as a consultant for the first six months." At the firm, "they really value finding out who you are and how you would fit in as a team member."

On-Campus Recruiting

Schools from which the firm actively recruits

Columbia
Cornell
Northwestern
Penn State
UCLA
University of Pennsylvania

Source: Towers Perrin and Kennedy Information/Consultants News

Compensation

TP's salaries are "probably not as lucrative as the McKinseys," but are "adequate enough when you consider the pros and cons that go with it like the flexibility, the culture, and the fact that you don't need to work around the clock." One consultant believed salaries firmwide were "below competitive." Starting salaries for MBAs are around the industry norm of $90,000; however, there are also signing bonuses and "deferred profit plans and year-end bonuses." Employee benefits include medical, dental, vision, domestic partner benefits, 401k savings, employee assistance program (mainly counseling), tuition reimbursement, retirement income, and profit sharing.

Office Life

People at TP are "the nicest group of people" and the firm is "very focused on valuing the balance between your work and home life." The firm's culture is "collegial and teamwork-oriented." A person is valued as an individual and "your opinion is respected; nobody is dismissed because of their level." There are frequent formal and informal outings, although two consultants mentioned that "partners rarely go." In New York, there are "dinners, picnics, and outings at the zoo."

TP has a billable requirement of 1,400 hours per year, which averages out to about 37 billable hours per week. This is "realistic and attainable," and the average consultant can expect to work between between 50 and 65 hours per week, depending on the engagement, though you may sometimes "pull an all-nighter." The real expectation is "to be an active contributor throughout the project barring extenuating circumstances." At the start of a project you are asked if you have the necessary time commitment. As long as they "can bring in someone to replace you, there is almost no problem" in changing your commitment to the project. The firm knows that "it's the quality of the work you do that matters and the billable hours that count." There isn't a "culture to work late" at the firm.

TP "isn't for everyone" because "most people out of B-school want to be a strategy consultant" and the firm's focus is in HR, which is "a component in strategy consulting." Also, if you want a place where the "work is assigned to you" this isn't your kind of place. You have to "find senior consultants to help you" and ask for work. If you do good work, they'll start coming to you. If you sit at your desk, "you won't get work." One consultant mentioned it was "like having your own little firm within a firm." Another consultant said organizational skills are a must; you must be able to juggle "several projects at once."

Geographic Locations

US Locations		Non-US Locations	
Atlanta, GA	Minneapolis, MN	Amsterdam, The Netherlands	Mexico City, Mexico
Austin, TX	New York, NY		Milan, Italy
Boston, MA	Parsippany, NJ	Bern, Switzerland	Montreal, Canada
Charlotte, NC	Philadelphia, PA	Brussels, Belgium	Newbury, UK
Chicago, IL	Phoenix, AZ	Buenos Aires, Argentina	Paris, France
Cincinnati, OH	Pittsburgh, PA	Calgary, Canada	Rio de Janeiro, Brazil
Cleveland, OH	San Antonio, TX	Canberra, Australia	Rotterdam, The Netherlands
Dallas, TX	San Diego, CA	Frankfurt, Germany	
Denver, CO	San Francisco, CA	Geneva, Switzerland	Sandown, South Africa
Detroit, MI	Seattle, WA	Hong Kong	Sao Paulo, Brazil
Hartford, CT	St. Louis, MO	Johannesburg, South Africa	Seoul, South Korea
Houston, TX	Stamford, CT		Singapore
Irvine, CA	Tampa, FL	Lisbon, Portugal	St. Albans, UK
Los Angeles, CA	Valhalla, NY	London, UK	Toronto, Canada
Miami, FL	Voorhees, NJ	Madrid, Spain	Vancouver, Canada
Milwaukee, WI	Washington, DC	Melbourne, Australia	

What Don't They Like?

The feedback process could use some fine-tuning; one consultant suggested there should be more frequent reviews than the semi-annuals currently used. Another consultant believed he didn't "receive any formal feedback in the first four months." Training, which, despite that it was described as effective, needs to be "timed better," specifically for new consultants, one person commented.

Firm Evaluations

MBA Perceptions of Towers Perrin (*1-5 scale; 1=poor, 5=outstanding*)

	Prestige/ Reputation	Compensation	Long-Term Career Opportunities	Quality of Life
1999 Rating	***	***	***	*****

Source: Kennedy Information Research Group's 1999 MBA Recruiting Study

Leadership Notes

John Lynch first joined the Towers Perrin Washington office in 1977. In 1979, he was transferred to the Pittsburgh office and became its office manager in 1982. He became manager of the New York office in 1986, and was elected a director of the firm in 1988. Lynch was elected president in 1990 and became chairman and CEO in 1991. He is a Fellow of the Society of Actuaries, and a member of the American Academy of Actuaries and the Conference of Actuaries in Public Practice.

Conclusion

Question: If there were any advice you would give a new consultant or a summer associate coming into Towers Perrin, what would it be?

"It's a self-managed career, so be proactive in managing it. Also, quality is definitely more important than quantity. Developing your relationships in the firm is critical."

— 27-year-old female consultant

"Come into the firm with an open mind, readiness to work hard, and have fun. Really try to have fun doing it and have a rewarding experience. If you come with the right mentality — open mind, willingness to work, and work well with others — you'll excel."

— 32-year-old male consultant

WATSON WYATT WORLDWIDE

at a glance

Year Founded:	1946
Headquarters:	Bethesda, MD
Key Players:	John Haley, President/CEO
1998 Revenue:	$720 million
Number of Consultants:	3,730
Web Page:	www.watsonwyatt.com
Recruiting Contact:	Sandra Ardenti, Corporate Recruiter
Address:	6707 Democracy Boulevard, Suite 800 Bethesda, MD 20817
Phone, Fax, E-mail:	Ph: 301-581-4628, Fx: 301-581-4937 E-mail:sandra_ardenti@watsonwyatt.com

About the Firm

Watson Wyatt Worldwide (WWW) was founded in Washington, DC in 1946 by Birchard E. Wyatt. In the beginning it was an actuarial and benefits firm, and is now the third largest HR consulting firm in the world. The firm officially became Watson Wyatt Worldwide in 1995.

WWW publishes hundreds of reports, newsletters, and surveys each year, covering the topics of people and business management, compensation, employee benefits, and risk management. The firm has expanded its global presence recently into places like Sri Lanka, Beijing, Bangkok, New Delhi, Sao Paolo, Mumbai, Johannesburg, and Zurich. WWW has strong branding in HR, is recognized worldwide, and has a series of imaginative advertisements in business magazines and newspapers that promote the firm's "sleeves rolled up" approach to consulting.

Services

WWW focuses on HR and strategy consulting. Its broad lines of businesses include Benefits, Human Capital Group, and HR Technology. Additional services provided through subsidiaries and divisions include: People Management Resources (PMR), Watson Wyatt Data Services, Watson Wyatt Investment Consulting, Watson Wyatt Software, and Wellspring Resources, LLC. The firm serves most industries and is particularly strong in healthcare.

The firm also offers the following services: Administrative Systems, Communications and Education, Compensation, Group Benefits and Health Care, Insurance Company, International, Investment, Organizational Effectiveness, Research Services, Retirement Program Consulting and Administration, and Risk and Insurance.

Career Paths

New associates join WWW practices with a focus in a specific area. Though they concentrate on a specific field, they work on "cross-practice teams" and get exposure to other areas as well. New associates are assigned to clients through their team leader, who has responsibility for the associate's career development.

WWW believes associates can better their careers (and their compensation) by "achieving professional excellence," which, the firm says, "occurs by a) mastering critical competencies, and b) consistently exceeding performance expectations." The firm also likes its associates to consider three "career development strategies" (Technical, Client, and Management tracks). The firm defines technical excellence as becoming "a master in a specialization." Client excellence recognizes "revenue generation and managing client accounts." Management excellence is "leading, developing, and managing."

Training

The firm has a one-week consultant orientation program called "The Business of Consulting" (BOC), which explains the firm's lines of businesses, services, and products. The initial training program "isn't a very strong one" but one consultant who was put on a rotational assignment got a "good hands-on perspective" of each of the three broad lines of business before she got into the Human Capital Group.

Summer Program

WWW offers summer programs on an "office-by-office" basis. Students who are interested in summer or intern opportunities should contact the regional staffing manager.

Recruiting
Number of Employees Hired 1998

	Actual (*academic yr. ending: 6/98*)
BA/BS	97
MBA	5
MA/PhD/Other Students	240

Source: Watson Wyatt and Kennedy Information/Consultants News

On-Campus Recruiting

Schools from which Watson Wyatt actively recruits

Baylor University	University of North Carolina
Brown	University of California, Los Angeles
Concordia University	University of Manitoba
Dartmouth	University of Nebraska
Drake University	University of Texas, Austin
Fuqua School of Business, Duke University	University of Michigan
Harvard	University of Minnesota
Iowa State University	University of Southern California
Kenan-Flager School of Business, UNC	University of Virginia
Ohio State University	University of Wisconsin–Madison
Pennsylvania State University	Wharton School,
Texas A&M University	University of Pennsylvania

Compensation

WWW consultants describe compensation as "competitive." One consultant said matter-of-factly that "I got what I asked for." The firm provides "pretty good vacation," starting out with three weeks a year and eventually increasing to five. The firm also "gives you a block of benefit dollars each year, in addition to salary," the precise amount depending on your status. You can purchase only the benefits you want, which works especially well "if you're single." Other firm benefits include 401(k), death and dismemberment insurance, and alternative work arrangements such as part-time, flex-time, telecommuting and job sharing, dental, life, medical, and tuition reimbursement.

Office Life

Overall, it's a very "energetic" culture with "a lot of young people here." People are generally "very supportive." Camaraderie comes from small groups of people around the office, usually the younger folks in their twenties. People who are new to the firm often get together to go out to lunch, but "the senior business types don't seem to do that." You travel four or five days a week when you are in the midst of a big project, but the average is "one or two days a week."

One consultant would only recommend WWW to certain types of people. "You have to be independent and know where you're heading," he commented. You also have to be able to "speak well and prove you know something and think on your feet," and be "free to travel." The firm could "manage its internal change process better," and when it comes to "devoting time, we could use our resources better." It can be hard to get on the projects you want when you first join the firm because "you're not proven." As with any firm, "it's not easy being the new consultant."

Geographic Locations

Major US Offices	# Pros (1998)	Major Non US Offices	# Pros (1998)
Atlanta, GA	55	Hong Kong	144
Bethesda, MD	197	Jakarta, Indonesia	50
Boston, MA	171	London, UK	130
Chicago, IL	178	Manila, The Philippines	52
Denver, IL	35	Melbourne, Australia	57
Los Angeles, CA	79	Montreal, Canada	80
Marlborough, MA	51	Reigate, UK	63
Miami, FL	22	Sydney, Australia	61
Detroit & Grand Rapids, MI	187	Toronto, Canada	154
Minneapolis, MN	109	Vancouver, Canada	86
New York Metro (New York, New Jersey and Stamford Locations)	161		
Portland OR & Seattle, WA	36		
Cleveland & Columbus, OH	136		
Philadelphia, PA	35		
Phoenix, AZ	56		
San Francisco, CA	142		
San Diego, CA	74		
Dallas & Houston, TX	158		
Washington, DC	272		

Leadership Notes

John Haley was given the president and CEO roles in January 1999. He succeeded A.W. "Pete" Smith in both positions. Smith became chairman of the board at that time and retired June 30, 1999, after a thirty-year career at Watson Wyatt. Smith is also a director of the Association of Management Consulting Firms. John Haley headed the Benefits Consulting Group at Watson Wyatt from 1997 to 1998. Prior to that, he was the global director for the retirement practice from 1996 to 1997.

Conclusion

Question: If there were any advice you would give to a new hire or a summer associate going into Watson Wyatt, what would it be?

"Get to know the right people, the ones who can get you on the projects you want."
— 28-year-old female consultant

The Authors

Michael Norris

Mr. Norris was an analyst at Kennedy Information (KI) for three years. His duties included providing research, analysis, and writing support for market intelligence studies and other KI publications.

He holds a B.A. in Sociology from Franklin Pierce College in Rindge, NH.

Giles Goodhead

Mr. Goodhead is a senior advisor at Kennedy Information and brings more than 10 years of experience as a global strategist to the position. Prior to joining KI, he held consultant positions at Monitor Company and Strategic Planning Associates (now Mercer Management Consulting).

Mr. Goodhead holds a Masters in Business Administration from Stanford University and a B.A. in Economics from Cambridge University.